D0970012

SEO
MADE SIMPLE

Second Edition

Strategies for Dominating the World's Largest Search Engine

by
Michael H. Fleischner

SEO Made Simple
(Second Edition)

Revised cover design by Marc Fleischner
Original cover design by Greg Wuttke

Library of Congress Cataloging in Publication Data is on file
with the publisher

ISBN-13: 978-1460908518
ISBN-10: 1460908511

Printed in the United States of America

To Jamie, Samantha and Alex-
My inspiration and joy

To my father, brother, and extended family

In memory of my mother

Contents

SEO Made Simple
2nd Edition

Foreword

A couple of years ago when I wrote the first edition of *SEO Made Simple*, I had no idea that search engine optimization would grow to become such an important part of everyday business. I've heard from hundreds, if not thousands of individuals and companies over the past two years searching for SEO secrets and solutions to their most pressing online marketing challenges.

The reason why search engine optimization has become so important is because the data on search marketing and buying behavior has proven time and again that organic search results drive significant amounts of qualified traffic to websites, blogs, and affiliate marketing pages.

At the same time, social media and personalized browsing experiences that integrate multiple forms of media into a single user session have become commonplace. The culmination of all of these factors has resulted in a growing demand for top search engine rankings and a better strategy for achieving number one results.

Not to mention that search engines are changing by the minute. Google Instant, universal search, suggestive type, multiple listings per site, social media integration, and other factors are reflective of the numerous ways we search online, and how the discipline of online search is changing.

Many of the individuals and companies I work with through my SEO business, *Upward SEO*, are not only interested in achieving top rankings for their websites, they're also concerned with online reputation. They seek top rankings for their sites and domination of the first page of Google and other major search engines.

This type of need has taken SEO to a completely new level. It used to be that success could come from optimizing a single web property. But now SEO is really about the optimization of multiple assets (websites, micro-sites, blogs, forums, social media, videos, press releases, and so on). That's why I felt so compelled to update this top-selling book.

Achieving your online goals requires the proactive management of your online presence in every sense of the word. Knowing the importance of doing so is the first step in achieving top rankings. With a thorough understanding of search engines, consumer behavior, and the importance of organic search, you're ready to learn SEO techniques that drive results for your business and protect your brand.

I'm often asked whether or not the search engine optimization techniques I first introduced a number of years ago are still a valid means for optimizing websites and other online assets. My response is emphatically, "Yes." Not only are the techniques that I'm going to share with you effective, they've grown in importance as search engine optimization has evolved over time.

In this updated edition, I have refined existing techniques and added new ones that make the most of social media, universal search, and other recent changes on the World Wide Web. However, the fundamental principals have not changed. Search engines like Google are still focused on one thing— a positive user experience.

Fast loading websites, valuable content, meaningful interactions, and authority, continue to drive search engine results. Sure, the Google algorithm is much more complicated than that, but I'm here to help you with all the particulars. If you start with an understanding that Google values a positive browsing experience, you're further ahead than most of the so-called SEO experts!

Introduction

If you want to rank on top for Google, Yahoo!, and other major search engines, you'll need more than just plain luck—you'll need the exact road map used by those who have already achieved top positions for their website(s). That's the purpose of *SEO Made Simple*—to provide you with a simple, easy-to-follow road map for achieving top search engine result placements for your very own website or blog.

I've personally read dozens of SEO books that left me without any practical advice or the guidance required to improve my website ranking. That was the motivation for this book. You won't find page after page of useless theory here. I wanted to create a helpful guide that would give you enough information to expand your understanding of SEO concepts and ideas, but place more of an emphasis on what to do and how to do it in order to see immediate results by improving your search engine rankings!

When I started out in Internet marketing, no one was able to show me how to achieve the results I was looking for. New to Internet marketing, the prospect of reaching the number one position on Google, or any other search engine for that matter, seemed next to impossible. Of course, there were marketing gurus and tons of Internet marketing products that offered "amazing results"; and I tried lots of them. In the end, many of these online products didn't live up to expectations. While trying to implement the advice given, I spent thousands of dollars creating and redesigning websites only to find that there was no single solution for getting top placements.

Although discouraged, I never gave up. I knew that in order to be successful online I'd have to increase the natural search engine placements for my website. Through a good deal of hard work and persistence, I discovered and refined the search engine optimization secrets I'm going share with you in this book. Now that I've achieved total search engine optimization success through years of trial and error, learning what truly works, I've decided to provide this information to as many individuals as possible seeking online success. Despite popular belief, you won't need an advanced degree in search engine optimization or years of experience in website development to improve your search engine rankings. All you'll need is a desire to have your website ranked number one on Google and a willingness to follow these simple, yet highly effective techniques.

How This Book Is Organized

In thinking about all of this information and how to present it, I decided to organize this book into two main sections: *On-Page Optimization* and *Off-Page Optimization*. Each section is designed to help you understand and implement the same techniques I've used to achieve top search engine placements.

Section 1: On-Page Optimization

The first section is an introduction to search engines and fundamental search engine optimization (SEO) techniques. On-page optimization covers everything you should do when developing your website and web pages. Don't worry if you've already spent money on designing your website or have limited knowledge of HTML or even website development itself. Once you know these techniques and understand how to use them, they can be applied in just a matter of minutes to any new or existing website.

Surprisingly, many of these techniques are overlooked by 98 percent of all Internet marketers and those who are attempting to improve their search engine result placements (SERPs). How do I know? I know because when my company *Upward SEO* reviews websites for clients, many of them aren't applying these basic SEO techniques.

At the end of this section, I'll provide a summary of the most important points covered concerning on-page optimization. You can use the summary page for quick review or as an ongoing reference to simplify your optimization efforts.

Section 2: Off-Page Optimization

The second section focuses on external factors that affect your Google ranking. These techniques are the most powerful and effective for improving your search engine results. In this section,

I'll discuss off-page optimization and reveal the very techniques I use on a daily basis to increase website popularity, a key factor in Google optimization. After applying these techniques in combination with section one, your website ranking will literally begin to skyrocket toward the top of Google and other major search engines.

It's important to note that I cover off-page optimization in the second section of this book because without on-page optimization factors being implemented correctly, your website can never achieve top placement (OK, *never* is an exaggeration, but it would take much longer and require greater effort).

Again, at the end of this section I'll provide a summary of its most important points for quick reference.

Section 3: Research to Practice

In this section I'm going to show you how to manage your off-page optimization efforts on a daily and weekly basis. This simple process keeps your website moving toward the top of Google and ensures that it stays there! Applying these techniques is the key to achieving results and protecting your top search positions.

Section 4: SEO Glossary

The final section of this book contains an updated SEO glossary that can serve as a helpful reference along your search engine optimization journey. By understanding key phrases and SEO language, you're sure to reach your final destination.

SEO Made Simple provides exactly what you need to begin your climb to the number one search position on Google, just as I have for many of my websites and blogs, and the websites I've developed and optimized for a long list of high-profile customers. As each page unfolds, and you learn the most powerful techniques for search engine optimization, you will achieve search engine success!

The Beginning

When I started learning about SEO, I really didn't know where to begin. And like most stories of challenge, I was at my ropes end—I had tried everything. After many sleepless nights, nearly $20,000 wasted on website development, and a lack of results, I was tired, frustrated, and broke.

After spending many endless hours learning how to apply the techniques that the number one ranked websites were using, I started using many of the same techniques on my own website and quickly reached the top of Google for specific keyword phrases. These findings resulted in what I am now calling the *SEO Made Simple* method. My focus was—and still is—Google, because it garners more search traffic than any other search engine. I've also learned that the optimization techniques used to reach number one on the world's largest search engine are unique.

Shortly after I began applying these techniques to my own website, I quickly went from being on page 10 in Google for key search terms to the top of the search engine result placements (SERPs). Although search engine results vary from time to time, all of my keyword searches show my website on the first page of Google, and many of them are in the number one or number two position.

Did you know?

According to recent studies, the top three natural search results on Google receive more than 65 percent of all search engine clicks!

After spending many late nights applying the SEO techniques I learned, it wasn't long before I developed faster, more efficient ways of getting results. These optimization techniques saved me valuable time and money, making the process much easier and faster to implement. I'll be sharing all of these techniques with you in the pages that follow so you can avoid wasting endless hours on manual processes that can easily be automated.

As a quick aside, let me show you the results I've been able to achieve with the *SEO Made Simple* techniques I'll be teaching you. Search engine optimization is all about optimizing your site for a given keyword. We'll be talking about keywords later in this book, but for now, all you need to know is that when you visit Google and search for something, the words you enter are comprised of either a single word or phrase. These words are called a *search term* or *keyword*.

Some of the keywords that I've optimized one of my websites (**MarketingScoop.com**) for include: *free marketing articles*, *marketing blog directory*, *Internet marketing expert*, and *marketing expert*. Even though the keywords are considered highly competitive, I've been able to achieve top placements using the techniques I'll be revealing in the first few sections of this book.

See these results below. They are unaltered screenshots from Google. Alternatively, you can visit Google and type in the keywords I've mentioned. Please note that Google SERPs can change slightly on a regular basis.

Keyword: *free marketing articles* I'm ranked number one here…

Keyword: *marketing blog directory* I'm ranked number one here too…

Keyword: *marketing expert.* Oh yeah, number one again!

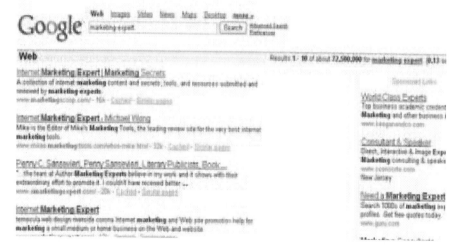

The best part of SEO is that I don't spend a single penny on Google Adwords or any other type of online advertising. Why would I? I'm getting all the traffic I can handle from the number one placement on the largest search engine in the world—Google! Other keywords I've focused on for this website include *marketing articles*, *marketing service providers*, and *marketing blog directory*. Feel free to check out my ranking on all of these keywords as well.

Here are just some of my traffic statistics for MarketingScoop.com, a direct result of being ranked first on a variety of search engines.

The best part about organic search results is that once you're in the top three placements on Google, the traffic just rolls in.

Monthly Totals [marketingscoop.com]

Date Range: 1/1/2010 to 12/31/2010

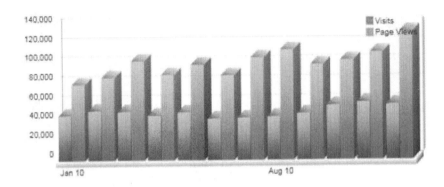

Take a closer look at these traffic stats and you'll see that some months I've attracted more than fifty-thousand visitors to my site— not bad for spending ZERO on PPC and other traffic generation programs!

I've reached top placements on Google with a basic understanding of SEO and SEO-related tools that give me an unbelievable edge over the competition who are trying to optimize for the same keywords and, in most cases, paying for their traffic.

What You Need to Know about Google

Google's the biggest—make no mistake about it. Global Internet information provider comScore, Inc., provides information on Internet traffic. According to comScore Media Metrix, using their qSearch service, which measures search-specific traffic on the Internet, Google sees more search activity than Yahoo! (#2) and BING (#3) combined.

Even though Yahoo's search engine results are currently driven by the Bing search algorithm, the amount of traffic each site represents online is minimal compared to search giant Google.

Below are figures about searching from comScore that were released to the public last year. The pie chart below shows the percentage of searches done by U.S. web surfers at home, work, and universities that were performed at a particular website or a network of websites.

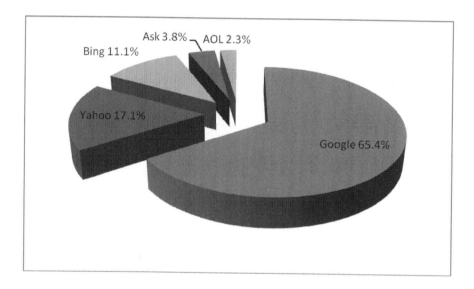

These figures are search-specific but not necessarily web search-specific. For example, a search performed at Yahoo! Sports would count toward Yahoo!'s overall total. Also note that some companies own more than one website. This means searches at different sites may be combined into one overall figure for the company's entire network. Here's some additional information:

- **Google:** Shows searches at any Google-owned website such as Google.com or Google Image Search.

- **Yahoo!:** Shows searches at any Yahoo!-owned website including AltaVista, and AlltheWeb.

- **BING:** Shows searches at any BING-operated website such as BING Search.

- **AOL:** Shows searches at AOL Search.

- **Ask:** Shows searches at Ask and any site within the Ask-owned Excite network.

Google PageRank Algorithm

What makes Google unique compared to other search engines is its proprietary website-ranking algorithm, also known as Google PageRank or Google PR. Named after one of Google's founders, Larry Page, Google PR is symbolic of the SEO industry.

Google PageRank defines the weight, or level of importance, that Google places on a given web page. I've heard many people try to describe Google PR in various ways, but I think the most simple is in the form of a voting system of sorts. What's different about Google is that the search engine is based on a huge voting system where websites vote for one another. How do they do this? Each link that a site places on its website, pointing to another website, serves as a "vote." Seems pretty simple, right? The more votes, the more important the website and the higher it appears in the search results! Well…sort of, but not exactly.

You see, in this special election, not all votes are created equal—some votes hold more weight than others do. For example, if a website with a Google PageRank of 7 (PR7) places a vote for a new website, that vote theoretically counts more than a vote from a website with a Google PageRank of 6 (PR6) or lower. So votes from different voters are weighted differently.

Said another way, it's not just the vote you're looking for—you also want a vote from the "right" person. In this instance, the "right" person is the website with the greatest influence (identified by a web page's Google PR and other factors). In my opinion, you're better off generating fewer links from sites that have a higher Google PR than many sites that have a low PR or PR of zero. You can determine your own website's Google PR by downloading the Google toolbar at http://toolbar.google.com and selecting the *Display Google PR* option. Once you load the Google toolbar, you'll be able to view the PR of any site you visit. The Google PageRank indicator can be seen on the right-hand side of the following graphic.

In addition to the Google PR indicator, when moving your mouse over the graphic, text will appear that says something like, "PageRank is Google's view of importance of this page (8/10)." You would then refer to the web page as having a "Google PR 8."

Many SEOs (people who make a living through search engine optimization) also believe that the relevancy of the link is a significant factor in the Google algorithm. In addition to getting votes from high PR sites, it may also be of benefit if those links are coming from authority sites in your field or website niche. Getting high PR links from sites in the "right neighborhood" may positively influence your rankings.

As someone who's done a lot of search engine optimization I believe this is a ranking factor but not critical to your results. Other factors that we'll discuss in this guide are equally if not more important to determining your ranking results. Keep in mind that search engine ranking algorithms combine hundreds of factors to determine where your site appears on a search engine results list. In fact, Google claims more than two hundred components to their ranking formula. I think it's safe to assume that relevancy and other factors play some role in how your site is ranked, given the scale and complexity of how rankings are determined.

Google Evolves

In addition to page rank and specific ranking factors, it's important to understand how Google search results have evolved. Search used to be simple. Buy a URL with your keyword in it and you were done. Over the past number of years however, Google has been focused on improving the search experience and has added a layer of complexity to search engine rankings like never before. In fact, they've added quite a few factors that influence results.

Universal search. With the advent of video hosting sites, blogs, and social media, Google has enhanced the search experience. A typical page of search results may include a popular video from YouTube, a news feed from a leading news site, and a relevant Tweet or Facebook comment.

This creates a more robust experience for those using the Google engine but requires proactive management for those interested in

SEO and online reputation management. Search engine optimization has become less about getting a single site ranked in the number one position and more about acquiring multiple listings on a search results page. As seen below, typical Google results display images, news, social media feeds, and more.

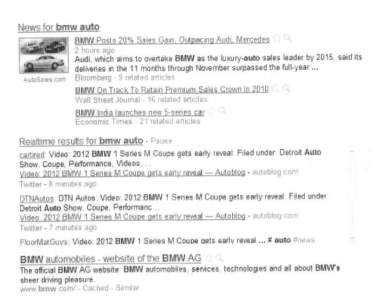

Due to the advent of universal search, search engine optimization has changed dramatically. Instead of just optimizing for a single website, I recommend applying all the techniques you'll learn in this book to any digital asset (press releases, social media profiles, videos, images, etc.). The more assets you optimize, the greater your presence on search result pages for a given keyword phrase. This takes additional effort but not much additional knowledge. When you understand the basics of search engine optimization you can use slight modifications to optimize virtually anything online.

Google updates. Upgrades to the Google interface have enhanced the user experience from start to finish. Google Instant, suggestive text, preview, and updates to Google Places means that users can access information more quickly and more precisely than previously thought possible.

In the past, Google would only give a website real estate in the top two positions for a given keyword. This has changed. If your website content is relevant to a user's search, you may be able to acquire multiple listings for a given keyword. Coupled with the fact that your video, news, and other media may appear if well optimized means that you can truly dominate the first page of Google, or any other search engine for that matter.

Understanding how Google has evolved is essential to getting and keeping your website ranked in the top positions for chosen keywords. In addition, Google offers many tools to help you along the way.

Google Webmaster Tools

Google is one of the most innovative companies on the planet. They actually want you to succeed. Why? Because they exist to improve search. To support this mission, Google has developed a number of tools you can use to "improve" your online search experience and website.

I use the term "improve" lightly because the tools do a lot from a diagnostic perspective, but don't do a whole lot when it comes to increasing your search engine result placements. Visit http://www.google.com/webmasters/ to view these helpful web tools. The webmaster's area on Google is referred to as "Webmaster Central" and is displayed below.

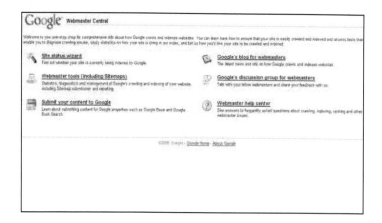

If your website is new, I advise registering at Google and using the Site Status Wizard tool and even submitting your content to Google via Google's Webmaster Tools to begin collecting valuable information about your website. Once you've accessed Webmaster Content, you'll be able to:

- **Get Google's view of your website and diagnose potential problems.** See how Google crawls and indexes your site and learn about specific problems Google has accessing it.

- **See how your site is performing**. Learn which queries drive traffic to your site, and see exactly how users arrive there.

- **Share information with Google to help them crawl your site better.** Tell Google about your pages—which ones are most important to you and how often they change. You can also let them know how you would like the URLs they index to appear.

Now that you know about the world's largest search engine and the tools they offer, it's time to start improving your website's Google ranking. These techniques can also help you improve your search engine rankings on Yahoo! and BING. After applying the techniques revealed in *SEO Made Simple,* you will see the most dramatic improvements in your Google rankings. With all the free traffic you'll be getting, concerns over attracting users from other search engines will fade away.

Section 1

On-Page Optimization

On-Page Optimization

As I mentioned in the introduction, there are essentially two parts to any SEO effort: on-page optimization and off-page optimization. We will begin with an overview and explanation of on-page optimization because it creates the foundation for your SEO efforts and is easy to understand. Simply put what you do on your web pages can have a positive or negative impact on your search engine result placements—where your site is ranked on Google for a particular search term or phrase.

What Is On-Page Optimization?

Defined in its most simple form, on-page optimization is what you do on your website to help or hurt your SERPs. From my perspective, on-page optimization also refers to critical planning steps like understanding your niche, keyword research, and web strategy.

The best part of on-page optimization is that it's fully in your control. If done correctly it can improve how search engines see your website, weigh your relevant content (keywords), and place your website within search results for a given term.

Many Internet marketers debate the importance of on-page optimization when it comes to Google. I believe that the effects of on-page optimization are more easily seen with other search engines like Yahoo! and BING when taken literally. However, I also believe that any Google optimization effort cannot be effective unless on-page optimization is thoroughly addressed at the start of your search engine optimization campaign.

What I'm referring to when I speak about specific on-page optimization factors is the proper use of *meta tags, website URLs, formatting, internal linking, keyword development*, and *on-page placement.* Let's review each item in detail after you learn about the importance of keyword research. I'll show you step-by-step what you need to know to ensure that your web pages are 100 percent optimized for Google and other major search engines.

Warning: Once you update your site with the proper on-page optimization tactics, you might very quickly find yourself ranked in the top five on some search engines like Yahoo! and BING. These particular engines, both of which are driven by the BING search algorithm, love on-page optimization!

Keyword Research

The more I learn about search engine optimization, the more I've come to rely on effective keyword research. Finding the search phrases that your website or blog should be optimized for is essential to any search engine optimization campaign. The goal is to find relevant, high traffic keywords that will be less competitive from an optimization perspective. Less competition means that you'll have a much better chance of achieving number one rankings for your chosen keyword phrase. Doing this takes a little work but is well worth it.

The value of selecting keywords strategically is very high. The "right" keywords allow your optimization efforts to happen quicker and produce the best organic result. Many of the companies I've consulted for over the past few years didn't pay much attention to keyword research. As a result, they were either trying to optimize their websites for keywords they could never achieve number one rankings for, because an authority site like Wikipedia held the top position, or for keywords that had next to no search volume.

Not too long ago I had a conversation with a potential client. We were introduced through a mutual friend and sat down to dinner to discuss his online marketing needs. I started to ask him questions about his online marketing strategy, website, and so on. About thirty minutes into the conversation, he said, "I don't need SEO. I'm already ranked number one for my keyword." When I asked him what the keyword was, which I'm excluding for privacy reasons here, I looked it up on my phone's web browser. I wanted to see how much search volume this particular keyword phrase had on a monthly basis.

Not surprisingly, the keyword that he was so enthusiastic about was getting less than four hundred searches per month. That's it! It's pretty difficult to build a business on only four hundred searches per month. He was surprised and said, "But in my industry that's how everyone refers to our service." I responded with, "That's clearly not the case."

After we started working together, I showed him the proper way to do keyword research and find the actual keyword phrases that people in his industry were typing into Google to find services like the ones he offered. With thorough research we found keyword phrases that his website could realistically rank well for in the short term and at the same time had enough traffic to sustain his business.

Before covering keyword research in detail, you must first understand the factors that are involved in proper on-page optimization and some off-page factors that influence website competitiveness. When I updated this book, I originally started with a complete chapter on keyword research but quickly realized that unless you have a firm understanding of the factors that influence rankings, you would never fully grasp the various components of effective keyword research. Therefore, we'll be covering basic on-page optimization components followed by a thorough overview and deep dive on keyword research.

If you already have a basic understanding of SEO best practices and are eager to start your optimization effort, you can always skip forward to the keyword research section which appears later in this book. Keyword research will be the place you start any optimization effort once you've acquired a fundamental understanding of SEO. Armed with this knowledge, you can choose the right keywords for optimizing your website, blogs, affiliate landing pages and other online assets, resulting in a very quick rise to the top.

Let's start with important on-page optimization factors and then I'll show you exactly how these factors will help you choose the right keywords for your website time and again. You can manage many of these on-page factors using your website editor (WISYWIG) or an html editor like PageBreeze, FrontPage, or Dreamweaver. If you don't have HTML experience, you can outsource this work but still need a basic understanding of what to do and how to do it. I cover everything you need to know about outsourcing later in this book so take a deep breath and relax. Effective SEO is easier than you think.

Meta Tags

A meta tag is any one of a variety of labels you give your web page. Although there are quite a number of different types of meta tags, we will discuss the most common ones here. These "tags" or labels are essential for helping search engines understand the name of your website's pages, know what information the pages contain, display a small description for search engine result listings, and understand how to treat each page when indexed.

Meta tags are important because different search engines weigh the information in these tags differently. It is believed that Google uses them in relation to other factors, ensuring consistency and validating page rank. It's good practice to make sure that your meta tags are complete, accurate, and up-to-date.

Note: Make sure that each page found on your website has its own unique set of meta tags. Duplicate tags can really hurt your rankings.

Here's an example of the meta tags I use to describe just one of my many websites, MarketingScoop.com:

<title>Internet Marketing Expert | Marketing Secrets</title>
<meta name="**Description**" content="Internet marketing expert reveals powerful marketing secrets. Search our internet marketing expert database, marketing service providers, and more.">
<meta name="**Keywords**" content="internet marketing, marketing secrets, online marketing expert, internet marketing help.">
<meta name="**Robots**" content="all">

You will notice from the example above that I've used four primary meta tags. These tags include the *Title* tag, *Description* tag, *Keywords* tag, and *Robots* tag. More meta tags exist but these are the basic ones you'll need to use when thinking about improving your SERPs. Let's discuss each one separately and make sure you understand how to create each individual tag.

Title

This tag is the page title. Not only does it tell a search engine what the main theme of your page is, it also shows up as the title of your website on a search engine results page. For example, using the title on the previous page you'll see that it appears as the highlighted title in the Google results (sample below). The title tag also shows up at the very top of your web browser for each web page you visit.

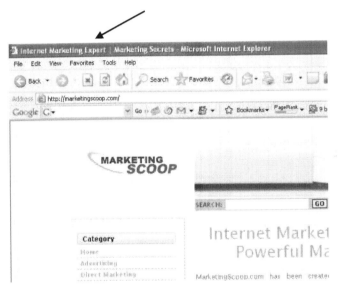

Internet Marketing Expert | Marketing Secrets
Internet marketing expert reveals powerful marketing secrets
marketing experts, service providers, and free marketing tools
www.marketingscoop.com/ - 18k - Cached - Similar pages

As a rule of thumb, make sure your title tag is *no more than seven words and less than sixty five characters*, including spaces. This is the maximum number of letters and spaces displayed as a Google title. If your title is longer, it will run off and include three trailing dots when appearing in the Google search results listing.

The reason you want to limit your title tag to only seven words is because Google places a weight (level of importance) on each word in your title tag. Therefore, the more words you have, the less weight applied to each word. This is why it's so important that your title tag contains the key theme of your web page or website and focuses on your specific keywords.

Note: Place your keywords in the title tag! I'll be covering keywords in the next section. For the time being, just remember that your title tag should include your keywords, as keywords are the terms your potential customers use when searching for you online.

I've used two keyword phrases as part of my title tag, separating them with a post (example: Internet Marketing Expert | Marketing Secrets). The post is found on your keyboard above the *enter* key. By separating these terms with a post, Google sees them as being separate and distinct phrases without taking up valuable title tag real estate. Keep in mind that by using up to seven words in your tag, you can develop many keyword combinations, mixing and matching terms. For example, my title tag has helped achieve first page Google placements for *Internet marketing expert*, *marketing expert*, and *Internet marketing secrets*.

Description

This tag provides a description of your website or web page. When you enter a description for your web page it will show up under the website title in the Google search engine results listing.

I like to use my keywords in the description tag twice—yes, two times! This has a direct impact on my SERPs in BING and related search engines. The impact to Google is minimal but does help with your overall optimization efforts. If you can, work your keywords into a description that seems natural and be sure to repeat your keyword phrase. Your description should be compelling and accurately describe what users will find when they click through to your page. This consistency is important to Google and the user experience.

Example of what to do:

> "*SEO Made Simple* can help you improve your **Google search results**. Read testimonials of those who have already improved their **Google search results** with these little-known Google secrets."

Example of what NOT to do:

"**Google search results**, **Google search results**, improve **Google search results**, buy this book to improve **Google search results**."

Overemphasizing your keyword phrase and stuffing your web page description can have a negative impact on your search engine results. Try to use your keyword phrase twice and no more. And be sure to generate a descriptive tag that compels browsers to click through to your website. This can provide a significant increase in the number of browsers who actually click through to your site from the search engine results page.

Keywords

The keywords tag is another way to educate search engines about your website. There are a variety of thoughts out there today about the importance of keywords and keyword tags. My belief is that keywords themselves don't carry significant weight in isolation, but analyzed in conjunction with the overall theme of your page, they signal Google as to the legitimacy of your content.

The keyword tag should include your main keywords, those you've chosen as the main focus of your website, as well as those associated with the theme of your web page (we'll be covering keyword research in just a few short pages).

Note: *Avoid keyword stuffing.* When users place keywords on their web page or within their meta tags over and over again in an effort to improve SERPs—search engines (like Google) actually discredit the value of the web page.

When listing keywords in their meta tags, some sites choose to separate each keyword with a space or comma. I prefer using a comma followed by a space to separate each keyword. Also, I like to make sure that I'm not repeating the same keyword consecutively. For example, if I was listing marketing-related keywords like *marketing, marketing resources*, and *search engine optimization*, I would NOT list them in that order because *marketing* is followed by another instance of *marketing* when I use the second term *marketing resources.*

The right way to list these phrases would be as follows: <meta name= "**Keywords**" content="marketing, search engine optimization, marketing resources">. This creates a division between like keywords, resulting in a more neutral approach and avoiding potential issues related to keyword stuffing. If you fail to implement this properly, some search engines won't fully index your page.

Robots

The simplest of all meta tags, the robots tag, signals the Googlebot, Google's search engine spider, to crawl your entire website. In order to index your website properly and include all of your web pages, search engines send their spiders to review and scan your website on a regular basis. Google does this every two or three days.

When the spiders view your meta tags and see that your robots tag indicates "all," they simply start crawling. Although some spiders would search the majority of your site without the tag, having it provides the added direction to search engine crawlers. Make sure the robots tag is included in your meta tags to improve crawling.

There are some Internet marketers or webmasters who recommend submitting each page of your site directly to the search engines via single page submission. This isn't necessary, especially if you are including the robots tag. Search engine crawlers do the work for you.

What's important is that Google indexes your site, and when it does, it can find all of your content. The robots tag can help with that process. Equally, if not more important, is compliance with W3C standards (industry accepted HTML standards) and a sitemap. When you combine the robots tag with an easily indexed website, Google and other major search engines can find and index all of the pages on your website or blog.

URLs

Many people believe that if you have a special URL, one that contains the keyword you're trying to rank highly for, you'll be number one on Google. **This isn't always true.** The reality is that having your keyword in your URL can help in some instances but is virtually meaningless in the overall Google ranking algorithm unless many other websites are linking to yours.

Let's explore this idea a little further. If this URL theory were correct, my site **MarketingScoop.com** would never be able to outrank a website like www.marketingexpert.com for the keyword phrase *marketing expert*. At the time of this writing, my site was in the first position on Google and the website www.marketingexpert.com wasn't even on the first three pages of search results.

So where does having your keyword phrase in the URL help? It helps with search engines like Yahoo! and BING and when you're link building for Google. Each search engine has its own ranking algorithm, placing different weights on website criteria like URL, external links, and more. BING is notorious for placing significant weight on the URL itself.

To see this in action simply go to BING and do a search for *marketing expert*. You'll see that the first five results, and those that follow, all have *marketing expert* in the URL.

Another way that having your keywords in the URL helps is when it comes to link building for Google. Each time a website links to your website using only your URL, if that URL is comprised of your keywords, it provides a boost to Google search results. As I'll show you later, all linking coming into your website should contain your keyword phrase, and this can be accomplished without owning a particular URL.

A great example of this concept is the keyword phrase "click here." Go to Google and enter the search term, "click here." If the URL theory was correct—that you have to own the URL that contains only your keywords—you would expect the first search result to be www.clickhere.com. However, the first result is for Adobe® Reader.

Why? It's because more sites link to Adobe Reader with the link text of "click here" than any other website.

All that said it never hurts to have your keywords in the URL itself. When others link to your site using just your URL, it will include your keywords. This helps when building links from sites that do not allow you to customize the link being placed or include your keywords in the anchor text.

Another technique that I have found to be particularly useful from an SEO perspective is buying aged domains. An aged domain is one that was established some time ago and may even have some traffic coming to it. You can search for and buy aged domains using GoDaddy or Sedo.com. If you can purchase an aged domain that already has your keyword included, all the better. This can give you a jump start when launching your website because it has been indexed by Google, likely has inbound links, and may currently rank for the keywords for which you're trying to optimize.

Formatting

The manner in which you organize and format your web page can have a huge impact on your SERPs. I'm going to show you how to make sure that Google and other major search engines are reading the text of your page prior to reading "other" page elements such as navigational items. Additionally, I'll show you where on your web pages to place your keywords and in what format.

Did you know?

You can see what elements of your page are viewed as text by leading search engines simply by visiting your website and pressing *Ctrl-a* on your keyboard.

There are a few basic things to keep in mind when formatting your website for top Google placement. The most important elements include *content first, clean code (W3C, no Flash), heading tags, alt tags, proper keyword placement, no Flash* and *JavaScript external,* and *sitemaps*. If you get these elements correct, you can move on to address additional optimization factors.

Content First

When I originally designed my website, I came to learn that the layout was completely wrong. Even though I had my meta tags in place at the top of my coded page, search engine spiders had to sift through my navigational items (which were JavaScript, not HTML) before they could reach my keyword-rich content.

A great way to ensure that search engine spiders read your text first is to lay out your site with the appropriate content at the top. Search engines read from left to right and top to bottom. Many websites have a left-hand column that contains navigation links. As a result, Google will read all of the text in the left-hand column before the main content area of your site. The preferred method is to have Google read the text from the main section of your page first so that keywords and other optimization factors are recognized.

In order to force Google to read the main content of your web page *before* the left-hand column, you need to structure your site appropriately.

Here's what you need to do (rather than creating a table to design your site):

navigational links	Your body text...

You should create a table that looks like this:

	Your body text...
navigational links	

By laying out your page in the format noted above, Google will read your body content *before* your navigational items. Navigational items often are constructed with excess code and, as a result, search engines are prohibited from reaching your optimized content. Here's an example of how to apply this technique using an actual web page.

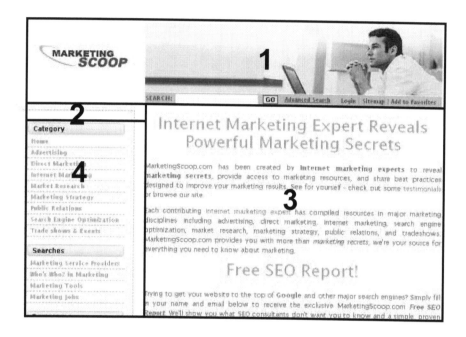

Proper formatting is essential for top placement in Google search engine results. If your site is set up incorrectly, the search engines will read your navigational items first, followed by your website content. As we discuss page elements and the importance of on-page items like <h1> tags and text formatting, you will better understand why we want the Google spiders to read your website content *before* all other page items.

Clean Code (W3C, no Flash)

As mentioned previously, I'm not a programmer, and, in fact, I know little or nothing about web development. But I do know there is a right way and a wrong way to design a website. How do I know? I learned my lesson the hard way—through trial and error.

Once I made the appropriate changes, my SERPs began to climb. That's how I discovered the importance of proper formatting and coding.

If you work for a company or have ever made a call to a customer support representative, you know that businesses operate according to specific standards and service levels. The same is true when it comes to web programming. When dealing with website code, these standards are referred to as W3C. The acronym W3C stands for the World Wide Web Consortium. You can learn more about the consortium by visiting their website at http://www.w3.org.

For implementation of proper SEO techniques, you should verify that your website meets these industry standards. When visiting the W3C website you can learn more about W3C and even check to see if your site code meets W3C standards by using their free validation tool at http://validator.w3.org. I recommend using this free tool that provides specific feedback as to which area(s) of your code meet standards and which do not. Run each key page of your website through the validator.

Any errors you encounter will need to be fixed by someone who knows the code in which your website was written. It is important for you to resolve the coding errors noted for a variety of reasons— not the least of which is that Google will have an even easier time evaluating your website.

Note: Be sure to use cascading style sheets (CSS) when developing your pages. This helps keep your code very clean. Instead of placing formatting code on the page itself, make a call to your CSS, which will allow you to reference all of the design-related elements you need across your website. Don't be too concerned if you're not familiar with cascading style sheets. Anyone who works in the area of web design has used them and can provide guidance when designing your site.

Heading Tags (<h1>, <h2>, and <h3>)

Heading tags (sometimes referred to as *headers*) are used to emphasize text on a web page. Search engines love to see these header tags because pages with large headings indicate the substance and importance of the content. Use the tag—either <h1>, <h2>, or <h3>—that's appropriate for your page and be sure to include your keywords in the tag.

For example: <h1>free marketing articles</h1>.

Using the <h1> tag will display your text in a rather large format unless altered via CSS. The <h2> tag displays text slightly smaller than an <h1>. The <h3> tag displays text smaller than <h2> and so on. Try to use at least one <h1> tag on the page you are trying to optimize.

Don't overdo it on your heading tags. One to three is sufficient. The key is to make it flow well with your page and appear natural. Placing tags that make your text appear unnatural will only hurt your website's readability and click-through rate.

Alt Tags

Do you use graphics or images on your website? If you do, each image should contain an alt tag. An alt tag is simply the practice of naming a photo, image, or icon. You can check to see if your website images already have alt tags associated with them by running your mouse over the image. If an alt tag is in place, text should display. If text does not display, an alt tag is not present and needs to be added.

The literal benefit of an alt tag is that the text displays while your website images are loading, giving users information about the content included on your page. The primary purpose for alt text is to ensure people with disabilities can read the page. Blind users who use a page reader cannot see an image. The alt text tells them what the image is. The secondary benefit (or primary SEO benefit) is that Google takes these keyword phrases into account when evaluating your website.

The best way to tag your images is with your keyword phrase followed by the word *image*. For multiple images, use slightly different wording. For example, if you're selling widgets and optimizing for *discount widgets*, you would include an <alt> image tag for your widget using the alt text *discount widgets graphic*.

The code that would be used to insert an image tag in this example:

```
<img src="widgets1.jpg" width="125" height="60" border="0"
alt="discount widgets graphic">
```

As with any optimization effort, don't overdo it with images or alt tags. Too many images can result in a slow loading website which is a key ranking factor. Images that contain a number of alt tags, all with your keywords, can signal keyword stuffing.

Proper Keyword Placement

You must focus on where and how your keywords are placed on your web page. The frequency of placement is less important than once considered. Many people believe that if they fill their web pages with nothing but keywords, they can attain top placement. Search engines have responded to this and actually penalize sites that over use keywords. The number of times your keyword appears on a given web page is called keyword density.

The concept of keyword density gets thrown around quite a bit in SEO circles. It refers to the number of times your keywords are used on a given page as a percentage of the total number of words. Most website gurus suggest a keyword density of 2 to 3 percent.

Today, keyword density has less of an impact than it once did on overall Google rankings. Of greater importance is the placement and treatment of your keywords. Use the following guidelines to optimize your page:

- Place your keyword(s) in the title tag, description tag, keyword tag, and alt tags.
- Place your keyword(s) in an <h1>, <h2>, and/or <h3> tag.
- Place your keyword(s) in the first twenty-five words of your page.
- Place your keyword(s) in the last twenty-five words of your page.
- Bold your keyword(s) at least once on your page.

- Italicize or underline your keywords at least once on your page.

Note: A great way to get keywords in the last twenty-five words is by adding it to your page footer after the copyright. For example, "© 2011 Your Site Name. Your Site Keyword." Adding your keyword phrase in this fashion is relatively natural and appears virtually unnoticed.

Following these guidelines for proper keyword placement shows Google that your keywords are important to your web page and your website. It also helps you compete with other sites that are not as well optimized using these on-page factors.

No Flash and JavaScript External

In addition to ensuring that your website code is up to standards, avoid Flash and JavaScript on your page. In my entire career, I have *never* seen a site that leads with a Flash intro rank number one on Google. If you can find one, I'd be surprised.

Flash intros do not provide keyword content in a manner that is easily searchable by Google. Even if the Flash intro was well developed and contained your keywords in some shape or form, the Google spider would not be able to read it. The whole idea of a Flash demo, which is a self-contained entity consisting of dense code is the exact opposite of what Google values. Google searches for open content that is readable and easily navigated.

Is all Flash bad? Only if your site is completely Flash based or your homepage consists of nothing more than a Flash presentation. If your intro page is largely Flash, I strongly encourage you to replace it with an HTML homepage. If Flash is still important, provide a link to your Flash script from your homepage. By doing so, you can optimize your homepage and then drive users to view your Flash demo.

JavaScript, a type of code often used for the creation of buttons, navigation, tracking, and so on, is another double-edged sword. Using JavaScript can improve a user's experience but at the same time, it can have a detrimental effect on your SERPs.

My recommendation is that if you would like to use JavaScript, place the code in an external file. This removes the majority of JavaScript code, helping your page load faster, and brings your most important content (meta tags, etc.) closer to the top of your web page.

Sitemaps

A sitemap is a single page on your website that provides access to all other pages on your site, at least the most important ones. Sitemaps serve two purposes. First, they make it easy for visitors to find content on your site, and second, they enable search engines to spider your site much quicker.

When the spider arrives at your website, it will read the first page of your site and then start looking at your navigational links (which include a link to your sitemap). When the search engine spider reaches your sitemap, it begins visiting and indexing each link contained on your map.

It's a good idea to have more than an index of links on your sitemap. Try to include short paragraphs of descriptive text for each link, which of course should contain your keywords.

You can create your sitemap in HTML. Doing so is easy and only requires an HTML editor. Your sitemap should consist of a single web page with links to your top-level pages.

Some search engines require an XML based sitemap. Creating an XML based sitemap isn't difficult at all. In fact, Google has made it easy for you with more free tools. You can get started with Google sitemaps and other webmaster tools by visiting Google at http:// google.com/webmasters/tools.

A number of free programs on the web (xml-sitemaps.com) can help you create an XML sitemap. Once you've created a XML sitemap that lists all of the pages on your website, upload it to your server and submit it to Google Sitemaps through the *Webmaster Tools* feature.

Note: Don't forget to update your sitemap every few months or so. Your site changes, and so should your sitemap—to reflect all of the changes you've made.

Uploading your sitemap to Google can have a positive impact on SERPs. Take the time to learn more about sitemaps, develop, and publish your own.

Internal Linking

One of the most important on-page optimization opportunities you have is to develop a simple and direct internal linking strategy. Internal linking refers to the linking structure your site uses to link to secondary pages on your website. How you link from one page to another is very important. Many sites significantly improve their rankings based on a strong internal linking strategy.

Internal linking provides direct access to your web pages in order of importance. The best practice for internal linking is to link to your main category pages from your website's homepage. To illustrate, I've created a fictitious website related to clothing.

In this example, the website's homepage is all about clothing and the types of clothing being offered for sale. From the home page you can access main category pages related to specific types of clothing. Once users navigate from the homepage to a given category they can read all about products, prices, and how to order individual items. To facilitate easy navigation, the homepage has links to each of the category pages.

Category pages may also be referred to as "top-level pages." The reason I use this label is because each of these pages is directly accessible from the home page in just one click. There are numerous benefits to this type of architecture which I'll be covering in more detail.

This would look something like the following:

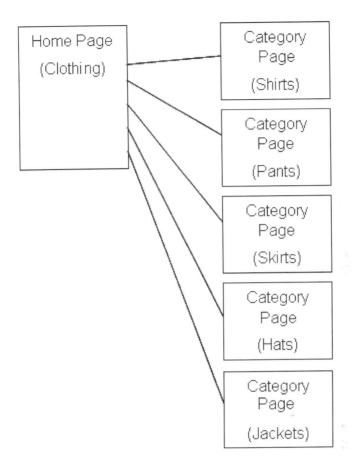

Although internal linking can be accomplished in a variety of ways, this is just one example of a basic linking structure you can follow. Here are some tips you can use to ensure your internal linking is designed properly:

- Include links to all of your main category pages from your homepage by placing links in a navigation menu. This menu should be available on each page of your website. Also, you can place links to your pages in your website footer (see **Sample 1** below).

- Include your keywords in the links where possible. This tells Google what content can be found on the other side of the link and reinforces your internal linking strategy.

- Don't place more than three links to the same page on your homepage. This is unnecessary and it could trigger potential issues with the Google search engine.

Note: Never underestimate the power of internal linking. Internal links are important because they allow for easy access to your content by search engine spiders and can transfer Google PR between pages.

Sample 1

Free Marketing Articles and more. To discover *marketing* secrets from an internet marketing expert or Search Engine Optimization Specialist, visit the Internet Marketing category.

Home | About | Press | Testimonials | Contact Us | Advertising | Direct Marketing | Internet Marketing
Market Research | Marketing Strategy | Public Relations | Search Engine Optimization
Tradeshows & Events | Service Providers | Who's Who? in Marketing | Marketing Tools | Marketing Jobs
Message Board | Marketing Glossary | Free Marketing Articles | Article Submission | SAFELINK Program
Logo Store | Careers | Terms | Privacy | Marketing Blog | Blog Directory | Link Exchange | Sitemap

This wraps up some of the most important on-page optimization factors you should be working with to improve website rankings. From meta tags to title tags and even internal linking, on page optimization is essential for top rankings. But did you know that no on-page optimization effort can be effective without considering what keyword phrases you are optimizing your web pages for? Let's change gears now and return to our discussion on keyword development. Once you fully understand keyword development you can ensure that all on-page optimization factors are created with your most important keywords in mind.

Keyword Development and Placement

Keyword development is one of the most important optimization factors you will learn about and it can make or break your website's ranking! But don't let that scare you. Now that you have a fundamental understanding of on-page ranking factors, I will show you the best way to find the right keywords for your website and determine whether or not you can rank well for them.

I mentioned previously that before we discussed keyword research and development, I wanted you to have a basic understanding of on-page optimization factors. This is because you want to optimize your pages around specific keywords and keyword phrases. Additionally, you'll want to focus on keywords when optimizing your site from an off-page optimization perspective as well.

Why are keywords so important? Because search engine algorithms are largely based on keywords—keywords on your web page, keywords in your code, keywords in the links within and pointing to your site. I guess you could say that Google and other search engines have keywords on the brain.

A keyword is any word or phrase that describes your website. Another way to think about it is in the form of a search term. What a user enters into the Google search box is considered a *keyword* or *keyword phrase*.

Let me begin by saying that choosing a keyword is more art than science. However, your selection of a keyword can be greatly simplified if you follow these steps:

1. **Define the content of your site in general terms.** What is my site about? Tennis shoes? Photography? Business services? Desserts? Once you've identified a general topic, it's time to start your keyword research.

2. **Identify keywords/keyword phrases related to your topic.** To do so, visit the Google Adwords Keyword Tool, which can be accessed directly or through a Google search at *https://adwords.google.com/select/KeywordToolExternal*.

You may be asking why we would use an Adwords tool for SEO, but you'll quickly discover the power of this free resource.

The Adwords tool looks like this:

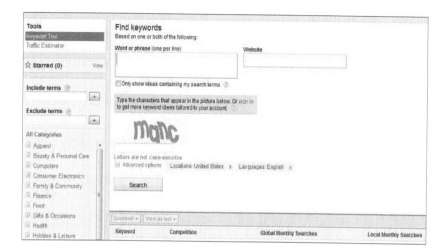

3. **Enter the keyword you're considering or the website you're analyzing, enter CAPTCHA code and press Search.** The resulting list contains all of the search terms and search counts—the number of searches using that keyword or keyword phrase performed during a given month on Google. Results are sorted by relevance but can also be sorted by search volume.

   Your results will look like the following screenshot including a laundry list of related search terms and corresponding search volumes. Google returns the local search results and global searches for a particular keyword phrase. Although both are valuable, I tend to rely more heavily on local results.

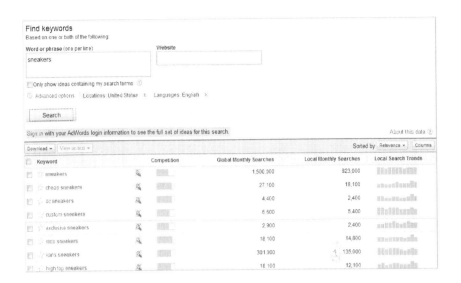

4. Select anywhere from ten to thirty keyword phrases to research further. OK, here is where the rubber meets the road. Look at your list and choose a few keyword phrases (not an individual word because, in most instances, it will be way too competitive with many sites trying to rank high for that particular keyword) that represent your website. Make sure your phrases have a search volume of at least three thousand monthly searches. Keep in mind that the more searches on a given keyword, the more competitive it may be.

Now you might be asking, "Why not pick the phrase with the greatest number of searches?" It stands to reason that the greater the number of searches, the greater number of visitors to your website. However, there are other factors to consider such as how competitive it will be to rank well for the given search term.

When I conduct keyword research I usually generate a short list by eliminating anything over fifty thousand searches per month and anything less than three thousand searches per month. I also eliminate phrases that appear unnatural or may be difficult to use in a sentence. This simple method usually gets my list down to about thirty keywords or so. Then I go to the next step to refine my search further.

5. **Commercial intent.** The concept of commercial intent has dramatically changed the Internet marketing landscape forever. Launched by Microsoft Adlabs, the idea of commercial intent is nothing short of miraculous. If you're already familiar commercial intent, then you know that I'm not exaggerating. If you haven't yet learned about this way of analyzing keywords, then you'll benefit from learning all you can about this one-of-a-kind analysis tool. Commercial intent measures the likelihood of transaction by keyword. To illustrate, let's look at the following example for the keyword phrase, "running shoes."

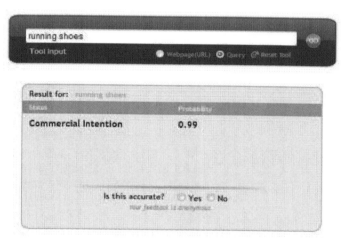

You'll notice that the commercial intent tool, found at adlab.microsoft.com/Online-Commercial-intention (or you can Google 'commercial intent tool') returns a commercial intent of 0.99. The closer the number is to 1.0 the stronger the commercial intent. The phrase "running shoes" has a very strong commercial intent meaning that the majority of users who search for this keyword phrase actually follow through and transact. A transaction may be an opt-in, clicking on an ad, or making a purchase. Although the accuracy of the tool is debated by some, I have had great success when researching keywords for affiliate products and SEO.

Now that you understand the concept of commercial intent, let's continue with our keyword research. Take your list of thirty or so keyword phrases and evaluate their commercial intent. You can plug each one into the Microsoft Adlabs commercial intent tool or find a resource online that allows you to grab the commercial intent of multiple keyword terms simultaneously. There are a variety of tools you can use that are either paid or free (some listed at http://MySEOmadesimple.com/secret.htm).

Before the commercial intent tool was available, the next best thing was to evaluate KEI. The KEI which stands for keyword effectiveness index is simply the number of searches performed on your keyword phrase divided by the number of sites competing for the same keyword.

You can find the number of competing sites/pages simply by searching for your keyword phrase in Google and looking at the total number of results noted in the upper left-hand corner of the search results page under the search box.

For example, if we were to choose the keyword phrase *women's tennis shoes* and do a search in Google, we would see that 865,000 web pages (at time of publication) contain the phrase *women's tennis shoes*. To generate the KEI ratio, we divide the number of searches, 6,600 by the number of competing sites, 865,000 and get .008.

Most SEO experts would look at this and say that this keyword phrase is "impossible" to rank well for because the KEI ratio is so low—less than one. *I would argue to the contrary.*

The primary reason is that 865,000 competing sites aren't that many in the grand scheme of the World Wide Web. I would say that any phrase that has over three thousand searches per month with fewer than three million competing sites might be worth optimizing for.

Why do I say "might be worth optimizing for?" It's because you need to do additional research to determine if the top-ranking sites are applying the *SEO Made Simple* techniques. If not, a well optimized site can outrank them.

Before moving on, be sure to analyze commercial intent, selecting keywords with a positive intent and eliminating those with a negative commercial intent, and then choose keywords with an adequate search volume of three thousand or more per month. Try to avoid search terms that have more than three million competing pages but don't use this as your only criterion.

6. **Research the competition.** Regardless of which tool you use to generate or research your keyword phrases, you'll need to size up your competition. This is the final step in keyword research and definitely one of the most important. Remember that Google is a voting machine. The question you need to ask yourself is whether or not you can optimize your website (both on-page and off) better than your competition and attract more votes!

Did you know?

There are a variety of tools you can use to research keywords in addition to the Google Adwords Keyword Tool. One of the most popular is called *WordTracker,* which offers a free trial version.

Researching the Competition

Researching the top-performing websites for final selection of your keyword phrase is the most important step in keyword selection and it takes a little work. The good news is that Firefox has a variety of plugins you can use to make your final analysis a lot easier. Plugins like SEO Quake provide much of the on-page analysis quickly, as opposed to doing all of your research manually—thank goodness!

After you've narrowed down your keyword list to just a few terms, the next step is researching the competition. I will now show you how to research the competition using a real-world example so you can do it for your own website. Keep in mind, there is software available that can automate this process for you (I've included a link on http://www.myseomadesimple.com/secret.htm).

Nonetheless, you should learn how to research your competition on your own to better understand this process of choosing keywords. Doing so is analogous to learning division longhand before you start using a calculator!

Picking up on our earlier example, assume you've selected a primary keyword phrase and have decided to begin researching the competitors (ex: *women's tennis shoes*).

1. Visit Google and enter the first keyword phrase you are researching. Enter the keyword phrase "women's tennis shoes" and select *Google Search.*

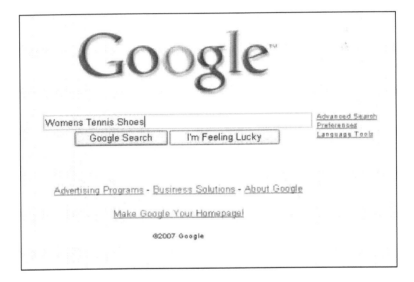

2. Identify the natural search results versus the paid search results. The natural results will appear below any paid results.

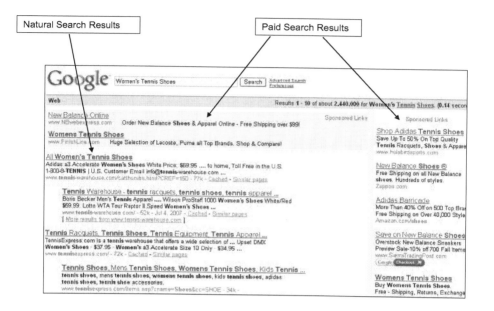

3. **Write down the URLs of the first set of natural search results**. The URLs will appear in green beneath each description. In this example, the first five natural results are:

- www.tennis-warehouse.com/catthumbs.html?CREF=150

- www.tennis-warehouse.com

- www.tennisexpress.com

- www.golfsmith.com/ts/browse.php?N=1548257

- www.zappos.com/n/es/d/35157.html

4. **Now you're ready to begin your site-by-site analysis.**

   You'll need to do the following for each site to determine if you can outrank them. I can show you how to do the first one—then simply repeat the same steps for sites two, three, four, and five. For each site, begin by recording the following:

- Website URL

- Google PR

- Number of sites linking in

- Keyword in <h1> tag

- Keyword in first twenty-five words of page

- Keyword in last twenty-five words of page

- Keyword bolded, italicized, and underlined

Let's do this for the first site:
www.tennis-warehouse.com/catthumbs.html?CREF=150

Begin by recording the Google Page Rank of this site. You can see from the rank meter in the Google Toolbar (you can download the Google toolbar at http://toolbar.google.com) that it has a Google PR of 4. You actually have to mouse over your PR checker in the Google toolbar to get the actual page rank.

The second thing we need to do is evaluate other on-page optimization factors we've discussed such as meta tags, use of <h1> tags, and so on. You can see from what I've circled that the title at the very top of the web page includes the phrase All *Women's Tennis Shoes* and the first header on the page says, All *Women's Tennis Shoe*s.

I also recommend looking at the source code and searching for <h1>, <h2>, and <h3> tags. To do so simply click on *Edit* in your browser menu, then select *View Source Code* and use the *Find* command. How many instances of header tags can you find?

Upon review, I noticed (see below) that the keywords are in the title but not in any <h1> or <h2> header tags. Additionally, I didn't find the meta tags that every site should have listing a title, description, and keywords—not to mention all the JavaScript that appears on the page—and this site is ranked number one. After some basic research, it appears as though the site we're researching isn't all that well optimized.

```
catthumbs[1] - Notepad
File  Edit  Format  View  Help
<html>
<head>
<TITLE>All Women's Tennis Shoes</title>
<LINK REL=StyleSheet HREF=http://rs.tennis-warehouse.com/tw/std.css TYPE=text/css>
<SCRIPT LANGUAGE="JavaScript">
<!-- //
function validator()
{
var good, j;
        good = document.appfinder.xcat.value != "";
        if (good == false) {
                alert("Please select an Apparel Type from the menu.");
                return false;
        }
if (document.appfinder.scode_color.value != "") {
        good = document.appfinder.scode_size.value != "";
        if (good == false) {
                alert("To use the color option, you must also select your size.");
                return false;
        }
}
}
// -->
</SCRIPT>
</head>
```

I did find an instance of the keyword phrase in an <h3> tag but it was pretty far down on the page of code.

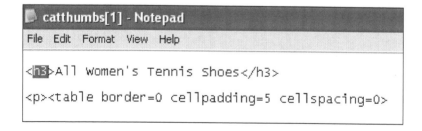

```
catthumbs[1] - Notepad
File  Edit  Format  View  Help

<h3>All Women's Tennis Shoes</h3>

<p><table border=0 cellpadding=5 cellspacing=0>
```

Note: You don't need to be an expert in programming code. All you're looking for is whether or not the website you're researching is using meta tags and header tags (<h1>, <h2>, or <h3>) that include the specific keyword phrase you're researching.

So what have we learned about this site? It looks to me as though they are not fully on-page optimized for the keyword phrase "women's tennis shoes" because they haven't followed all of the on-page optimization techniques we've covered in the first part of this book. This is a positive sign because if we chose to develop a competitive website, we could use meta tags and other on-page techniques such as <h1> tags, bolded text, internal linking, proper keyword placement, and a fast loading page, to enhance Google optimization. Lastly, the Google Page Rank of 4 is good, but over time, we could match it or even beat it with a PR5 rank.

See what I mean when I say that just because a site is considered "competitive" it may still be worth competing against using search engine optimization? With the application of proper on-page and off-page SEO techniques, you could certainly out-rank this website for the keyword phrase "women's tennis shoes." All it would take is some time and proper application of the *SEO Made Simple* techniques.

Final Two Factors

Even though we haven't focused on off-page optimization just yet, there are two more factors you need to consider before selecting your final two to three keyword phrases. I only recommend two or three keywords per page because, as you'll discover in the next section, if you focus on more than a few phrases, you won't be able to apply all of the necessary on-page factors needed to influence search results.

Factor 1: Google Page Rank (a.k.a. PR). We've already touched on the concept of Google PR, but it's worth mentioning as a key factor in your final selection of an ideal keyword. Google Page rank is a measure of a page's importance on a scale of 1 to 10. A site's level of importance is based on a variety of factors including age, number of inbound links, quality of inbound links, and many other factors. However, it's easy to understand that the more important a page is, in the eyes of Google, the better it will rank for particular keywords. Your goal is to find a keyword where the top ranked sites have low Google PR.

You can determine a web page's Google PR by loading the Google toolbar into your browser and navigating to any website or blog. The Google Page Rank of that particular web page will be displayed in the Google toolbar. If it does not appear, visit the options section of the toolbar and make sure you've selected Google PR as a toolbar element. The higher the PR, the more difficult it will be to outrank this particular website. When I'm researching a possible keyword, I always look to see what the Google PR values are for the sites currently listed in the first, second, and third positions on a search result page. If the top sites have very high Google PRs (6 or more), I generally move on. Trying to outrank sites with that much importance takes time and resources.

Factor 2: Inbound Links. Google loves links. As noted in the previous paragraph, Google places a lot of emphasis on inbound links as well as other factors like the authority of those links. We'll discuss authority, age, inbound/outbound link ratios, and more, in the off-page optimization section later in this guide. For now, simply know that the more third-party sites that are linking to any particular website or blog, the more strength that website carries. In essence, each inbound link is giving a site "juice." The more juice, the more value, importance, and significance a site has and the more difficult it will be to outrank.

For example, if I compare a make-believe website called site A, which only has two inbound links vs. site B which has three hundred inbound links, site B will have more relative strength, assuming that the quality of the inbound links are the same. As a result, site B will rank higher for a given keyword if optimized properly. Inbound links are a key indicator of competitive strength.

As a final step to your keyword research, complete Google searches for each of your final keyword phrases and analyze the sites in the top few positions. Do they have really high PR values? How about a large number of inbound links? Try to find the search terms that have little competition. If you can find a keyword where the top ranked results have low PR values and few inbound links, then a top ranking for your website or blog is just around the corner.

Did you know?

A significant factor in the Google algorithm is page load speed. Based on testing and analysis, I found that top ranked websites tended to load more quickly than other sites competing for the same keywords. In addition to applying all of the on page factors discussed in this section, evaluate how quickly your web pages load using free web-based tools compared to other websites.

Section One Summary

Here's what you should take away from this section about on-page optimization:

✓ On-page optimization is what you do on your website to influence SERPs on Google.

✓ Doing proper keyword research is the first step to a successful SEO campaign.

✓ Having proper meta tags is essential. Always include your keyword phrase(s) in your meta tags.

✓ The proper meta tags include your title tag, description tag, keywords tag, and robots tag.

✓ Choose your URL carefully. Your URL doesn't have to have your keyword included but it helps when other sites link to your site using only your URL.

✓ How you format your page is important for optimization purposes.

✓ Make sure you design your web pages so Google is forced to read your on-page content first.

✓ Verify that your code is W3C compliant.

✓ Don't forget to include your keyword phrase(s) in <h1>, <h2>, and <h3> header tags. This signifies the importance of your content to Google.

✓ Label each graphic with an alt tag that includes your keyword phrase.

✓ Place your keyword(s) in the first twenty-five words on your web page and the last twenty-five words on your web page.

✓ Italicize, bold, and underline your keyword phrase within your content.

- ✓ Eliminate Flash if it's the main presentation of your website. Google does not view this favorably.

- ✓ If you're going to use JavaScript to enhance the overall visitor experience of your website, place the code in an external file.

- ✓ Focus on a fast loading website. This is essential for top Google rankings.

- ✓ Be sure to include a sitemap that's easily accessible by Google.

- ✓ Never underestimate the power of internal linking. A good internal linking structure can improve your SERPs.

- ✓ Keyword development is one of the most important on-page optimization strategies.

- ✓ Research keywords and competing websites to select ideal keywords.

- ✓ Research the strength of the competition before selecting your final keywords using PR and number of inbound links.

- ✓ Page load speed is a significant factor in Google rankings. Ensure that your home page loads more quickly than those of competing sites.

Section 2

Off-Page Optimization

Off-Page Optimization

As I mentioned in the introduction, there are essentially two parts to any SEO effort: *on-page optimization* and *off-page optimization*. Off-page optimization is even more powerful than on-page optimization when it comes to increasing your search engine results on Google. In my experience, about 85 percent of your results are directly correlated to off-page optimization.

In fact, after years of consulting for large companies, I've proven that it's possible to achieve positive results without actually applying on-page optimization if using off-page techniques properly. However, going down the path of skipping on-page optimization is a difficult one. Achieving the results you want will take much longer and require a lot more work. Always begin your search engine optimization with on-page optimization to expedite results.

Now that we've discussed the importance of starting with on-page optimization, it's time to focus on the next step of any effective SEO campaign—off-page optimization.

What Is Off-Page Optimization?

In its simplest form, off-page optimization can be referred to as increasing a website's popularity. This popularity is defined by the number and types of websites that link to a given website or URL. I also like to think of off-page optimization as what you do on the Internet, *not* directly on your website, to improve search engine result placements.

The best part of off-page optimization is that there are a handful of proven techniques you can start using today to improve your SERPs on the world's largest search engine.

Off-page optimization is the most important SEO strategy for those seeking number one placement on Google. The fastest and most effective way to achieve this goal is by developing quality links to your website. When I refer to "quality," I'm referring to links from sites that:

- Have an equivalent or higher Google PR than your site

- Include similar content to your web page

- Use related meta tags

- Come from diverse sources

- Have a large number of quality sites linking to them!

Even more important than the *what* (quality websites) is the *how*. Specifically, how these quality websites link to you is an essential key to Google dominance.

Did you know?

Your success on Google is DIRECTLY correlated to off-page optimization—the types of websites that link to you and how they are linking to you.

This is the biggest secret to Google dominance. Using this "secret" has changed my failure into success. Let me give you some visuals to reinforce the point.

Let's begin with a search for the term "marketing article." You'll notice that the first search result is for the page of my website that includes my original marketing articles. This page is located at **MarketingScoop.com/articles.htm**. The keyword phrase "marketing article" is a highly competitive one with about 267 million other pages containing the same phrase. You can see this by looking in the upper right-hand corner of the Google search results page. You can also look for derivatives of this term as well, such as "marketing articles," which has eighty-seven million competing pages.

The second and third listings on the page are for Marketingsource.com and marketingarticlelibrary.com. Why is my site ranked first? The answer is simply that I have better quality sites linking to my website in the right way. It's really that simple because I've taken care of my on-page optimization factors.

Everything

Images

Videos

More

Saddle Brook, NJ
Change location

Any time
Past 24 hours

All results

▸ Free Marketing Articles | Marketing Articles
you don't change the free **marketing article** in any way; you include the byline ..... Article
Marketing Your Key to Improved Search Engine Rankings ...
www.marketingscoop.com/articles.htm - Cached - Similar

Article Library - marketingsource.com Articles Library
The marketingsource.com **article** library contains thousands of articles on topics of interest
business owners, **marketing** professionals, and much more. ....
www.marketingsource.com/articles/ - Cached - Similar

MARKETING ARTICLE LIBRARY- Sales, Advertising, Internet Marketing ...
CLICK HERE NOW TO VISIT OUR BLOG Marketing Article Library™ .... 2010 **Marketing**
Article Library™ All rights protected. Use of our free service is protected ...
www.marketingarticlelibrary.com/ - Cached - Similar

Let's take a quick look at the websites linking in. This will give us a better understanding as to why my website is ranked in the first position. Anyone can do this by typing the following into the Google search box—you've gotta love Google!

Link: www.yoursitehere.com

Be sure to replace "yoursitehere" with your website or the URL of the website you're researching and press enter. There are a variety of ways to get a more complete listing of inbound links to a particular website or page, such as Yahoo! Site Explorer and other tools, but for the time being, let's rely on the data that Google provides.

Below you'll see a listing of all the sites Google has identified as linking into my website page **MarketingScoop.com/articles.htm**. In the upper left-hand corner you'll notice the number of inbound links but more importantly, beyond those from my own site, they are quality links from high Google PR sites.

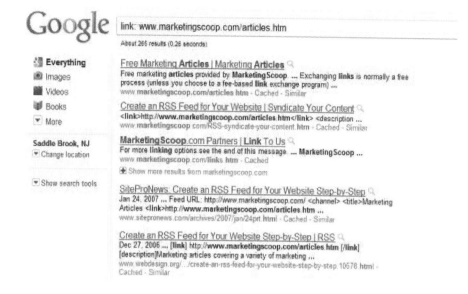

According to this result, Google tells me there are 265 links pointing into this page on **MarketingScoop.com**. Gee, I wonder how this compares to the number two ranked website for the keyword phrase "marketing article." Let's take a look at the results:

There are 9,370 links pointing in. How could this be? One would assume that more is better right? Not so. As I mentioned previously, it's not about link quantity. Rather, your rankings have more to do with link quality than anything else. This site has more than nine thousand links compared to my 265 but they are mostly internal links and from sites of poor quality. Strive to attract links from well established, authoritative, third party websites if you want to improve your ranking.

I know the screenshot here is small, but if you look at the first result, you'll notice that the title has something to do with Forex Trading. This certainly isn't relevant, and quite honestly may be seen as somewhat spammy by Google. Additionally, take a closer look at the link itself. This isn't a third-party link but rather an internal link from the same website. Taking it a step further, most of the links pointing to this page are of poor quality and aren't passing the necessary authority back to the primary page. Said another way, the inbound links are pretty worthless.

Now, let's take a look at our third example, *Marketingarticlelibrary.com*. Logic would dictate that the owner of this site would have fewer sites linking in than the first site, fewer than the second site, and so on. With that in mind, let's take a look.

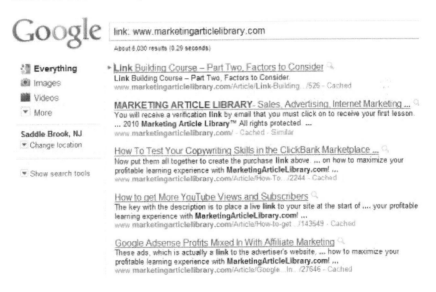

More than six thousand sites are linking into this website. Similar to our last example, many of the links are internal (using other link evaluation tools we'd be able to filter these from the results). Additionally, many of the sites linking in are either not of very good quality or are not referring to marketing articles in their link text.

If all of the sites linking in use link text that says something like *click here* versus *marketing article*, their search engine value to Google is extremely low for the search term *marketing article*. This is why I stress the importance of how external links are designed when pointing to your website. **They must contain your keywords when possible**.

Furthermore, it's possible that many of these sites have a Google PR of 0. To find out for sure, you'll need to use an online SEO tool or software program (tools for further analyzing competing sites at http://MySEOmadesimple.com/secret.html). Again, it all comes down to *link quality*, which is a function of Google PR, content alignment, sites linking into the linking site, and link text.

Achieving top rankings for your website is based on a combination of on-page factors, the quality of inbound links, link authority, and text.

Link Types

Before going any further, let me explain the various link types. There are really only three types of links you need to know about: *one-way links*, *reciprocal links*, and *three-way links*.

- **One-way links.** These are links from a website that is not your own. Also referred to as third-party websites, these sites place a link from one or more of their web pages to your website.

  Google values one-way links above all else. One-way links are incredibly powerful (if they're quality links) because you are receiving a vote from an independent third party.

- **Reciprocal links.** When you exchange links with another website, commonly referred to as *swapping links*, you're providing a link to their site (from your own) in exchange for a link from their website to yours. Reciprocal links are valuable, but not as valuable as one-way links.

- **Three-way links.** Three-way linking is when you partner with another website (site B) and provide a link from your site (site A) to their site. In turn, they provide a link from another site they own (site C) back to your site. It looks something like this:

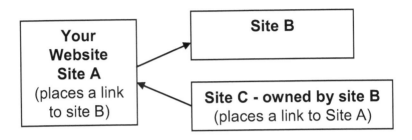

This form of link building is ideal because it results in a one-way link from a third-party website.

From Which Sites Should You Be Getting Links?

Now that you know the importance of links, the first question you must ask is where you should be getting links from. There are a variety of strategies to apply here.

The most effective way to identify the "right" sites to get links from should be based on who is linking to your competition, which is defined by who outranks you on Google for your identified search term. This is a very important strategy and one that is frequently overlooked. You should be evaluating who links to the number one search result in Google for the keywords or keyword phrases you're optimizing for and try to acquire links from the same websites.

Did you know?

If you get the same sites to link to your site in the right way, and you've optimized your site properly, in time you will outrank your competition on Google for the same given keyword phrase.

Many methods help you determine which sites are linking to the number one result in Google for the keyword phrase you're targeting. Begin by identifying which site is in the first position for your search term. You can do this by visiting Google and typing in your search term. Record the URL of the number one search result. Once you've identified this site, do one of the following:

- **Google search.** Go to Google.com and type in the following: *Link: www.nameoftoprankedcompetitor.com* and press the return key. Then, replace the phrase, "nameoftoprankedcompetitor.com" with the name of the site you've identified as having the number one position on Google for your search term.

  The result will be a series of sites linking to your competitor. The only downside to this method is that you won't know which sites are more important than others (e.g., the number of links linking into those sites, Google PR, keyword content on pages, etc.), but it will certainly identify the sites you need to target for link-building purposes.

- **Alexa.** Go to http://www.Alexa.com and type in the name of the site you're researching. Alexa.com is a tool used to measure the popularity of sites based on the browsing activity of those who have downloaded the Alexa toolbar. Because not everyone uses the Alexa toolbar, the information is only directionally correct but provides a reasonable starting point as well as additional websites you can target with your link-building campaign.

  Once you get the resultant websites, you'll see a number of options listed for each one. To the right of your competitor's website thumbnail image, click *Sites Linking In*. This option returns a list of sites that Alexa has identified as linking into the site you're researching. Use this list to target sites for link building.

- **Online SEO tools.** I have found that using online marketing tools to automatically generate a list of sites linking into your competitor's website, as well as link details such as Google PR, link text, page title, and so on, can be the most effective way to generate a list of targeted sites for your link-development efforts.

  I've personally bought and used about a dozen different products to help me keep an eye on my competition and, more importantly build an effective linking campaign. I regularly use SEO software because in less than thirty seconds, I know exactly which sites are linking to the number one positioned website for my target phrase and receive information that helps me prioritize my efforts like the Page Rank of each inbound link and domain age. You can learn more about the software packages I use at mySEOmadesimiple.com but keep in mind that using online SEO tools aren't always necessary. You can often accomplish the same outcome without purchasing SEO software. However, these tools save you a significant amount of effort, reducing the time required for acquiring in-depth link-building information.

  You can use whatever SEO or link analysis software you want as long as it provides you a list of sites linking into your competitors and a way to prioritize that list. If you start to develop links from the highest quality sites first, your climb to the number one spot on Google will happen that much faster.

- **Identify authority websites**. Authority websites are those sites linking to three or more of your competitors. If you don't have a SEO tool at your disposal, you can accomplish this manually using the following method:

  1. Search for competitive sites by visiting Google and searching for your most important search term.

  2. Create a spreadsheet of the top one hundred sites "linking in" to each of your top five competitors (Microsoft Excel is a good tool for this).

  3. Sort alphabetically.

4. While looking at the list see if any of the website URLs are duplicated across your list or use the "find" function. If the site appears two or more times, highlight it.

5. Once you've developed your list of authoritative sites, visit each one to determine how your competitors are listed and how you can acquire a link to your website.

Model the strategy your competitors have used. If these sites are directories, look for a directory submission form. If the links are from articles that your competitors submitted, submit your own. If all you can locate is an e-mail, ask the webmaster to include a link to your site. You may also suggest a link exchange if the opportunity arises.

If the website is already linking to your competition, they are a prime target for a link exchange or for adding your link because they see value in linking to sites covering similar subject matter.

The fastest way to achieve top rankings is to try to get links from the same sites that are linking to the number one, two, and three top search results for your desired keyword. You won't be able to get links from all of them and, in fact, may only be able to get a few, but each inbound link can benefit you.

After applying the competitive link strategy, the next step is to build quality inbound links to your website through a variety of ways that we'll be covering in the next few sections of this guide. Before I reveal the most effective link acquisition strategies, you must first understand the proper way to format an inbound link for maximum results.

How to Link

Now that you know how to find the sites you want to receive links from, you need to learn the proper way to develop a Google-friendly link. Google-friendly links are links that improve the search engine results of a given website. This is one of the ways that I've been able to get much better rankings for my web pages even though I may have fewer links pointing to my site compared to competitors.

I always cover the formatting aspect of linking in detail because your links are virtually worthless if they're not displayed correctly on other websites. Let's begin with the anatomy of a link; for example, let's take a look at http://www.marketingscoop.com.

As a web browser, you would likely look at this link, know it was a link, and click on it if relevant to your search. This common application of link design is pervasive throughout the web and used consistently (blue and underlined). Another way to present the same link is with alternate link text. For example: Marketing Expert

Link text can also be referred to as *anchor text* and is essential for Google optimization. Embedded behind the link text is an active URL. In the example above, if you were on a web page and positioned your mouse over the *Marketing Expert* link, you'd see the URL of http://www.marketingscoop.com embedded within. It is recommended to use link text instead of your URL text whenever possible.

The question I often get is, "If you're trying to get links to your website from other sites, why wouldn't you want them to simply place the URL of your website on their website?" There are a number of important answers to this question.

1. Your search result placement on Google is DIRECTLY correlated to the quality of the links pointing to your site *and* their link text.

2. A link that says http://www.yourcompanyname.com doesn't tell users anything about your website or why they should visit your website unless you're a well-known brand. How can you expect to drive traffic if no one knows about or has ever heard of your website? Even if your URL is somewhat descriptive, you're better off with informative link text that includes your keywords.

Note: If all you did was develop a link-building campaign and asked third-party websites to place your URL on their sites (example: www.marketingscoop.com), you would improve your

Google ranking for your website name only (example: marketingscoop) and nothing else. Remember, you're not trying to rank well for your own URL, you're trying to rank well for a given keyword phrase.

To rank on top for a particular keyword or keyword phrase, you want third-party websites to place your link with the proper anchor text on their website. Your anchor text should include your keyword phrase (example: <u>Marketing Expert</u>).

When users search Google for the keyword phrase "marketing expert," as noted in the example above, it's my website that shows up in the search engine results list because Google finds many links pointing to my website that say *marketing expert*. Go out to Google and do a search for "marketing expert" and you will find my website, MarketingScoop.com, ranked in the first position. This is because I've used anchor text, which included my keyword phrase, to build lots of quality inbound links to my site.

One thing to keep in mind is that you may want to vary your link text from time to time so Google doesn't think you're up to any funny business. Although it's not essential, adding some variety is good for all involved—browsers, webmasters, and website users. One way to do this is to use multiple keyword phrases in your link text.

Using an example from the section on keyword research and title tags, you can vary your link text by using more than one keyword phrase. For example, in addition to including *women's tennis shoes*, we can add another keyword phrase like *Nike tennis shoes* and separate with a post (example: <u>Womens Tennis Shoes | Nike Tennis Shoes</u>). The post is usually found on your keyboard over the *enter* key. The result is that each time you get your link placed on a third-party website, you're actually optimizing for two keyword phrases instead of one! The HTML code you can use to get this effect, if you're not using a WISYWIG editor, is as follows:

<a href="http://www.yoursitename.com" title="womens tennis shoes" target="_blank" rel="dofollow">Womens Tennis Shoes | Nike Tennis Shoes</a>

As always, be sure to replace http://www.yoursitename.com with your own website URL and obviously use the appropriate title including your keyword phrase. I also like my links to open in a separate window (a.k.a. target= "_blank") and be marked as "dofollow". This tells search engine spiders to follow the link back to my site. When engaging in reciprocal link exchanges, three-way link exchanges, or if simply requesting a link from a site, provide them with the link formatting noted above.

Make sure that every time a website links to you they are using the specific linking format (using anchor text that includes your keyword[s] or keyword phrase[s]). I can't tell you how many times possible link partners have asked me for a link exchange and submitted their link to me in the traditional link format, example http://www.sitename.com.

Even though these potential link partners are on the right track in terms of developing inbound links to their website, they'll never achieve Google dominance because they aren't asking me to place their link using their desired keywords as the link text. Applying the proper link formatting to your inbound links is vital to the success of your search engine optimization efforts.

How to Get Links to Your Website

As I mentioned earlier, building links to your website is the most important aspect of improving your Google search results—bar none! It also provides a significant boost to improving your search engine result placements on other search engines like Yahoo! and BING.

When I started out, I never realized just how important inbound links were to Google or how to acquire quality links to my website in the right way. As a result I spent thousands of dollars, not to mention years of trial and error, to figure out that the more quality inbound links I developed, including my keywords in the anchor text, the higher I'd get listed on Google.

When thinking about acquiring inbound links, and those links pointing to your website from other websites, there are two key principles to keep in mind.

Principle #1: Quality attracts quality. When it comes to search engine optimization, if you take the time to do things right the first time, you will achieve your goal. An example of this would be the process of asking a related website for a link that includes your keyword phrase(s). If you send a form letter or brief email and ask for a link exchange, you probably won't get it. However, if you take a few minutes to look at the website you're targeting and identify an opportunity to deliver something of sufficient quality (content, reciprocal link, etc.) you'll likely receive what you're looking for.

Principle #2: Persistence pays off. As I teach you the techniques I've used to rank number one on Google for even the most competitive phrases, think back to this principle again and again. Persistence is the key for achieving your desired result. A great example of this is some work I was doing for an online service company. After analyzing their website and suggesting some changes, I quickly realized that my on-page optimization recommendations would never be implemented—largely due to a bureaucratic web development team and their inability to handle multiple projects simultaneously. Over time I have found this situation to be more the norm than the exception.

Despite an inability to implement my on-page suggestions, I moved forward coaching the marketing staff of this company on the off-page optimization techniques for improving Google search engine result placements. They immediately started implementing these techniques on a regular basis to help their site increase rankings for specific search terms.

Truthfully, nothing happened for about eight weeks...and then WHAM! The techniques they used for building links to their website took hold and the results were undeniable. One of the keyword phrases that was most important to them went from the bottom of page 2 on Google to the number six position—even without the benefit of on-page optimization.

Today, everyone is looking for a quick fix. When it comes to SEO, there are a number of quick fixes out there. These concepts are often referred to as *black hat* techniques and more often than not, they result in getting your website banned from all the major search engines. Achieving top search engine placements is like losing weight. If you go on a starvation diet, sooner or later you're going to gain back all the weight you've lost and then some.

On the other hand, change you're eating and exercise habits slowly over time and you can create lasting health. The same principle applies here. Develop your links with a focus on quality, quantity, and diversity. Once you achieve top placements, you're likely to stay there with little additional effort. Be persistent and you will achieve lasting results!

SEO Made Simple Off-Page Techniques

Let's jump right into it. All of these off-page optimization techniques will help improve your Google SERPs through link building, the most effective search engine optimization strategy available today. The more you use these link-building techniques, the faster you'll see results. Don't hesitate—start using these off-page optimization techniques immediately to build quality links to your website and watch your Google search engine results start the climb to the number one position.

Article Marketing

Article marketing is the practice of writing informational articles within a given subject area and distributing your articles to information-hungry websites across the web. A number of article distribution sites will distribute your articles to webmasters seeking content. This is done by registering with an article directory, adding your article to the relevant category on their site, and submitting it for review.

Once the article has been reviewed and approved, it is posted on their website for webmasters to copy and paste onto their own websites. **You leverage this *SEO Made Simple* method by including a link back to your website in the *About the Author* section using the proper link text (which includes your keyword phrase[s]).**

Each of these article distribution sites allows you to include an *About the Author* section at the conclusion of your article (see example on next page). You can see that I embedded multiple links back to my website at the end of this sample article.

Sometimes the author section has a header that says *About the Author* and other times it just appears at the end of the article. Don't submit an article without it.

In the following example, I embedded two links, one for *marketing blog directory* and the other for *marketing blog*. Embedded in each of these links is a URL that points back to my website(s). For fun, see where my website MarketingScoop.com ranks for "marketing blog directory" as identified by the first instance of anchor text and where my blog (http://marketing-expert.blogspot.com) ranks for "marketing blog" as noted by the second link. You'll see top placements on Google for each of them!

your home page, you want them to interact with your site. Be sure to optimize your home page for SEO purposes, ease of use, and interaction. Creating a positive user experience will get visitors to return again and again.

*Michael Fleischner is a marketing expert and the president of version-next.com. Visit today for free marketing information and marketing blog directory. Michael has more than 12 years of marketing experience and had appeared on The TODAY Show, Bloomberg Radio, and other major media. Visit his marketing blog for further details.

Back to Top

The added value of article distribution is that in addition to getting links to your website from the article site itself, you also get the *viral effect* provided when others post your articles.

The *viral effect* is when a webmaster takes your submitted article from the article distribution site and uses it on his website or blog including your author box. Over time, his web browsers may point to the article on his site or copy and paste the article onto their own websites or blogs if reprint rights are offered, generating even more one-way links back to your website.

To see the true effect of article marketing, search on Google for one of my many marketing articles, "7 Proven Strategies for Improving Your Alexa Ranking." You'll find more than two thousand references to this article, many of which are from quality websites. The result, because many of these sites have my Author Box included at the bottom of the article, is more than two thousand one-way links pointing to my website with a single article! It's like link building on steroids. Each link builds my link popularity and is essential for improving Google search results. The best part is that this link-building activity costs me little or nothing to implement.

What if you don't have anything to write about?

If you are struggling to write your own articles, there are plenty of tools out there that can help you create a unique article. If you're not in the market for this type of software, you can also hire a ghostwriter or freelancer. I would recommend finding someone through eLance.com or Getafreelancer.com. You could likely negotiate with someone depending on your topic and pay as little as $10 per article.

Writing original articles or having original articles written for you can be worth *every* cent! Overall, article marketing has created thousands of links back to my websites. In fact, if you Google my name *Michael Fleischner,* you'll find tens of thousands of references. Most of these references are directly associated with my article marketing, one of my favorite SEO strategies.

I have evolved my article marketing techniques over the past few years to save time while improving effectiveness. Additionally, changes in how content is viewed by search engines like Google has modified the way I use this strategy.

It is widely reported that Google is penalizing sites for publishing duplicate content. Regardless of the accuracy of this statement, it's important that you find ways to create unique content. A good habit to get into is to first publish your article to your own website or blog before distributing to third-party article directories and sites. This gives you claim to the article as your own. Once you begin distributing the article, make sure that each submission is unique. Doing so increases the chances that your article actually gets published online and provides the "link juice" you want from it.

The challenge with unique content is that even if you have an original article and publish to your own website, that article is no longer unique. What happens when you start submitting to third-party sites? How can you create unique content each time you submit an article? The answer to that question is a concept called

Article Spinning. Spinning an article means that you use a tool to generate multiple unique articles from your existing content.

You can write your own article and then create multiple, unique versions of that article, before submitting to article directories. There are a variety of spinners on the market that help you with this process. I recommend using a spinner if you are manually submitting to article directories just as I did when I started building links to my sites manually.

Now I prefer article marketing services that can distribute unique articles to hundreds of targeted websites and blogs on autopilot. Spinning and submitting articles on your own can take hours or even days. Thankfully, there are a small number of reliable tools that can take your article, once versioned properly, and distribute it on autopilot. What's nice about the tool I personally use is that you can pace the distribution of your content. This ensures that links aren't built too quickly, resulting in the Google slap.

The key to link building is to establish inbound links to your site in a slow and steady manner. Tools that help with article distribution generally submit a large batch of articles all at once. When I found a tool that would allow me to set the rate at which I distribute articles, I was in heaven. This tool has become a standard for anyone interested in improving search engine rankings!

For a list of article writing resources, including automated tools and services to write, spin, distribute, and track your article marketing, visit www.myseomadesimple.com/secret.htm.

To get you started, here is a list of some of the most popular article directories to which you can submit your articles. There are hundreds more, but these are some of the most popular. Don't forget to spin your article multiple times to create unique submissions to each of the following article directory websites.

1.   www.Goarticles.com

2.   www.eZinearticles.com

3.   www.ArticlesBase.com

4.   www.Buzzle.com

5. www.ArticleAlley.com

6. www.Webpronews.com

7. **www.ArticleSet.com**

Place Free Articles on Your Website with Reprint Rights

Another way to optimize your own content is to post your authored articles on your own website with reprint instructions (I suggest doing this before submitting to article directories). This allows your website browsers to repurpose your content under specific terms and conditions and search engines to recognize you as the original author—a very important step for improving search engine rankings.

Create a single page on your website that lists all of your articles. On this page, provide instructions on how your articles can be used. For example:

You're welcome to reprint these articles on your website and in your e-newsletters free of charge, provided that you don't change the article in any way and you include the byline (including a link to our website).

In doing so you agree to indemnify [your website name here] and its directors, officers, employees, and agents from and against all losses, claims, damages, and liabilities that arise out of their use.

Note: *By viewing and copying the source of this article, you'll be able to retain all formatting.*

In addition, or in lieu of the message above, you may want to repeat a similar disclaimer at the footer of each posted article. For example:

Publishing Rights: You may republish this article in your website, newsletter, or book, on the condition that you agree to leave the article, author's signature, and all links completely intact.

Article marketing is one of the fastest and most powerful ways to build links to your website. Again, remember that you want quality links, so take your article writing seriously. I suggest creating one to two articles per week and distributing them to at least twenty-five to thirty article directories. This can increase your SERPs both short and long-term.

Whether you use a service to author articles for you or do your own writing, always strive for unique content (40% or more of an article) and pace your distribution. Over time, this is one of the most powerful tactics for building tons of quality inbound links to your website or blog.

Link Exchanges/Link Requests

One of the fastest ways to build links to your website, and therefore link popularity, is through *reciprocal linking*. As we discussed in an earlier section, there are essentially three types of links: one-way, reciprocal, and three-way. One-way links are the links you acquire that point directly to your site. We are discussing a number of methods for acquiring one-way links, such as article marketing, because they are often the most powerful type of link you can acquire. Reciprocal links are created when two websites agree to link to each other. Reciprocal links are also known as *link swaps, link exchanges*, and *link partners*. When I was first starting out in search engine optimization I used reciprocal linking to establish a number of quality links to my website.

The challenge here is that a reciprocal link is really only valuable if the Google PR of the site that's linking to you is greater or equal to the Google PR of your own website. That's not to say that links from sites with a low PR don't provide value. In fact, when you're starting out, every inbound link with a Google PR greater than zero helps!

In the last couple of years, basic reciprocal linking has fallen out of favor. Although I don't necessarily agree that there's no value in a link exchange, I do believe that you need to use a combination of link-building strategies if you ever wish to achieve top search engine placements for your desired keyword phrases.

When you're developing reciprocal links, seek out websites that are contextually relevant to yours. In other words, if your site is about clothing, seek out other sites dedicated to apparel. These sites will tend to have similar content (keywords) to your site embedded in title tags, body copy, on-page links, and so on.

Google favors links from sites that share the same or similar theme as your website, increasing the value of each incoming link. The more time you spend seeking out relevant link partners, the better.

Reciprocal Links and How to Get Them

Before asking any site for a link exchange, you'll need to develop a links page on your own website. A links page, also referred to as a partner page, is where you'll be placing the links to those sites that place one or more of your links on their website. As a rule of thumb, never include more than one hundred links on your links page, as Google may consider your page to be a link farm. Link farms are in the business of posting links to other sites for a fee. And most importantly, **place a link to your links page from your home page**.

Linking from your home page will transfer the Google PR of your home page, which usually has the highest Page Rank of any page on your website, to your links page—making it all that more valuable to potential link partners.

After you've created a page to place links, it's time to find some link exchange partners. Begin by identifying a site that would be an appropriate link partner (see **From Which Sites Should You Be Getting Links?**). E-mail the webmaster of the site by locating a *Contact Us* button or form or the webmaster's e-mail address.

Before you send an e-mail requesting a link exchange, place a link to the targeted website on your links page. Doing so shows the webmaster of the site that you're serious about a link exchange and willing to take the first step. If the webmaster says no, you can always remove their link from your links page. Here is a sample e-mail you can use when contacting webmasters:

> Dear Webmaster,
>
> My name is _____ and I am the webmaster of PUT YOUR WEBSITE URL HERE. I have visited your site www.theirwebsiteurlhere.com and believe it would be a valuable resource for my website browsers.
>
> I'd like to exchange links with you and have already added a link to your website on my links page at www.yourlinkspage.com. I would ask that you provide a link back to my website. Doing so would offer a valuable resource to your website's visitors and increase website popularity for both of us.
>
> If you are interested in exchanging links, please add the following details to your website and let me know when you

have done so. The details of our site are given below:

Title: Your keyword phrase here | Second keyword phrase
URL: www.yourwebsite.com

Description: [Place a description of your website here. Make sure you include your primary keyword phrase at least two times in a manner that seems natural]. Alternatively, you can just copy the html code

<a href=http://www.yourwebsite.com target="_blank">Your keyword phrase | Second keyword phrase</a> *Place a description of your website here. Make sure you include your primary keyword phrase at least two times in a manner that seems natural.*

If you are not interested in completing a link exchange at this time, please let us know and we will remove your link from our links page. Thank you for your consideration.

Kind Regards
[your first name]

Feel free to modify this e-mail as you like. The key is to sound genuine and act in good faith. As I mentioned in Principle #1, quality attracts quality and in #2, persistence pays off. You'll receive more no answers than yes answers, but over time yeses add up and you'll have plenty of quality links to your website!

Based on the type of website, and how well established your site is, you may consider sending a link request without the promise of a reciprocal link. A one-way link is more valuable than a reciprocal link, but websites aren't always willing to provide you with one unless they see you as a well-established authority website.

On a final note, once you establish a link exchange, check back regularly to make sure the reciprocal link is in place. If your link has been removed, contact the webmaster to inquire as to why your link was removed. Keep in mind that you want the value of the inbound links to your links page to be greater than the value of the outbound links; always make sure a reciprocal link is in place or remove the site from your links page.

Three-Way Link Exchange

The next type of link exchange is called a three-way link exchange. As noted in the previous section, "Link Types," a three-way link exchange is similar to creating a one-way link to your site by offering a link to someone else's site in return. This can be handled in a similar manner to our reciprocal link exchange—sending an email to the webmaster defining your intentions. I can tell you definitively that if you spend the time to find a relevant site and have a secondary asset (another website or blog) you can use to generate a one-way link to your prospective link partner then three-way links may be a great strategy for you.

The key to being successful with link exchanges is always to think value and relevance. Try to acquire links from third-party sites in your niche that have authority in the form of high Page Rank, Age, or number of inbound links. Relying on three-way link exchanges isn't going to produce top rankings over night, but used in combination with other strategies, it is a relatively quick way to generate quality links pointing to your main website.

Directory Submission

If you're going to own and operate a website, you must take the time to submit your website to well-established website directories. There are tons of websites out there called website directories that list other websites and website details. Directory submission is a great way to generate hundreds of one-way links to your website.

Some directories may charge you to be listed in their directory of sites. This fee is often used to pay an editorial staff to review and post your listing, but it may also serve as the price of getting your link posted on a website that has an established Google PR. In essence, you're buying page rank. The one thing to keep in mind is that Google reportedly penalizes "paid links." As a result, you want to limit the number of links you acquire through paid directories.

There are two types of website directories on the Internet: *human-edited* and *automated*. Human-edited directories review each submission by hand. These directories are of high quality and command a top Google PR. The most popular of all human-edited directories is DMOZ.com. In fact, even Google uses DMOZ for the Google Directory at http://directory.google.com/.

Automated directories are basically a dime a dozen. I don't mean to diminish the value of these directories, but you certainly have to make sure you get what you pay for. Even if a directory submission is free, you want to focus on submitting to *quality* directories—sites with an established Google PR, strong Alexa ranking, appropriate categories, and so on.

Another aspect to consider is that many human and automated directories work on a concept of link exchange. To get listed in their directory, you must provide a link to the directory from your website. In this situation, you should first check to see the PR value of the page in which you will be listed. Only submit your website to the directory if the Google PR of the page (where your website will be listed) is equal to or greater than the PR of your links page. That way, you receive greater benefit in terms of link equity and create value for your site. If you attract links with a lower PR, you do not obtain any real value.

Start your directory submissions with the largest free directories:

DMOZ
DMOZ is a huge directory that's used by many other websites and managed by a system of volunteer editors. Please note that it can take a long time to get your site listed.

www.dmoz.org/add.html

Google
There is no charge for any site to list. Google finds your site whether you manually submit or not, but it's definitely worth letting them know you're there.

www.google.com/addurl

Yahoo!
Non-commercial sites may be submitted for free consideration. Commercial sites require an annual payment of $299.

http://search.Yahoo!.com/info/submit.html

Fee-Based Directories (There are thousands, but these are the ones I recommend.)**:**

Gimpsy (Free/Charge: $30 one-time fee)

This is an interesting directory with a slightly different layout. Free listings have a long waiting period.

www.gimpsy.com/gimpsy/searcher/suggest.php

JoeAnt (Charge: $39.99 one-time fee)

This is a directory run by volunteer editors.

www.joeant.com/suggest.html

GoGuides (Charge: $39.99 one-time fee)

This is a directory run by volunteer editors.

www.goguides.org/info/addurl.htm

There are other well-known directories like "Best of the Web" and "Aviva" but they charge upwards of $79 to be listed. You're more than welcome to spend the money, but I suggest you exhaust all other link-building strategies first.

One of the best ways to find free directories to submit your link to is with directory submission software. I've used a variety of them to make the task of finding and submitting to hundreds of quality directories more efficient. Alternatively, you can seek out websites that list free web directories. I've provided such a list on my website http://www.marketingscoop.com/website-directories.htm. I've also used a free site called One Way Text Link to help me manage my manual directory submissions. The site keeps track of submissions and is available at http://www.onewaytextlink.com/.

Blogging

Blogging provides SEO value from two distinct vantage points. By now you know about blogging and maybe even have a blog of your own. From a search engine optimization perspective, having your own blog provides a significant boost to your SEO efforts over time. I'll also show you how to leverage other people's blogs to build inbound links and increase your search engine rankings.

Let's begin our review of how to use blogs for SEO purposes by talking about setting up your own blog. Although creating your own blog isn't necessary, it does have a number of benefits that can't be overlooked. Once you create your own blog and that blog earns a positive Google PR, you can start adding links and passing authority to any site you choose. For example, a number of years ago, I started "The Marketing Blog," which is now ranked number one on Google for the term "Marketing Blog." Anytime I launch a new website or want to give a client some extra link juice, I simply make a post to the third-party website. Essentially, by creating your own blog you are developing an authoritative resource you can use to pass authority and value to any site you are optimizing! This is a great long-term strategy that comes in handy when you want to quickly increase the rankings of new websites you are trying to get to the top of search result listings.

A number of years ago, after hearing about the popularity of blogs and learning about the multiple benefits of creating one, I set out to start my own blog. By doing some research, I found a number of popular websites that actually let you create and host your blog for free. What's even better is that the process of creating your blog is incredibly fast and easy. I suppose that's why blogging has become so popular.

Step 1: Choose a Purpose or Topic

One of the most important things you can do to ensure a quality blog is to determine the purpose and the topics you will be writing about. For example, a number of individuals who host blogs simply want to share their ideas on a particular topic. Others are looking for an outlet to make posts on just about anything without a real agenda. Often these latter individuals are seeking to create an online journal or even generate revenue with Google AdSense (pay-per-click advertising), advertising, or promotion of affiliate products.

Regardless of the purpose you choose, select a topic that allows you to contribute on a regular basis. You'll often develop ideas for the next post based on comments readers submit. This is one of the best ways to develop new content that is relevant to readers and keeps them engaged.

Step 2: Select a Blog Provider

There are a number of websites that offer free blogs. The two largest and easiest to use are Blogger.com and WordPress.com. These sites have millions of users and have been offering free blogs for a long time. The benefit of using established blogging hosts is reliability and functionality. I personally use Blogger.com for my marketing blog where I offer a variety of search engine optimization tips and information at http://marketing-expert.blogspot.com. I've also launched a number of blogs using WordPress which is now the blogging standard. You can host a WordPress blog on your own site (WordPress.org) or use their hosted service (WordPress.com). If you're not sure which to use I suggest you visit YouTube and start watching videos related to blog setup. There you can get some insight into the different blogging platforms that are available.

Step 3: Launch Your Blog

If you're selecting Blogger.com to launch your blog, all you do is create an account, name your blog, and choose a template. From there you can begin posting to your blog immediately. Many providers like Blogger.com give you the ability to choose from a number of basic templates. Advanced users can design their own blog templates to customize look and feel.

WordPress.com, another blogging tool, is also very simple to use. After creating a username and entering your e-mail address, you create a blog name and title. You'll receive a confirmation e-mail that provides instructions on how to begin.

Once you've launched your blog and made a number of posts, you should really focus on generating traffic. Not only will traffic support any online business you may have, but it can also improve the overall quality and Google PR of your blog. Some simple techniques for generating traffic to your blog include:

- Register your Blog with DMOZ, Google, and other blog directories (Technorati, etc.).

- Design your blog for SEO using on-page optimization techniques.

- Generate links to your blog via link exchange, article marketing, and traffic exchanges

- Update content on a daily or weekly basis.

- Use ping services like Ping-o-Matic to recognize new posts.

One thing you'll find about starting your own blog is that blogging is both simple and fun. As you develop a loyal readership, you'll find blogging to be a great learning experience as well. Simply put, there's no reason why you shouldn't start blogging today. Once your blog is up and running, place a link from your blog's homepage to the website you are trying to optimize, including the keywords you are optimizing for. This will obviously help your Google ranking via the inbound link-building strategies we've been discussing, but you should wait until your blog has an established Google PR before linking out to other websites. This can take a number of months.

Blog Commenting

The second way to use blogs effectively for search engine optimization is through the concept of blog commenting. When you visit a blog, most posts give you the option of leaving a comment. This may be available by clicking on a hyperlink that says "comments" or simply beneath the post itself. Blog commenting is a great way to acquire a one-way link to your website.

The first step is to find high authority or high Google PR websites in your niche. It's important that the blogs you leave comments on are what we call "do follow" blogs. This means that the blog owner permits third-party links to be indexed by search engines, passing value from its pages to your website. To find valuable do follow blogs, you can use automated blog indexing software (resource listed on my secret page www.myseomadesimple.com/secret.htm) or by searching Google for "High PR Do Follow Blogs."

Once you have created a list of high PR, do follow blogs, you can begin leaving comments on appropriate posts. Here are a few tips for making the most of this strategy:

1. Enter your keyword in the field marked, "Name." This is the MOST important step in productive blog commenting.

2. Use a real email address for submission purposes.

3. Use a complete URL when listing your site address in the space provided. Do NOT include a URL in the actual comment.

4. Leave a comment that is directly related to the post, has substance, and is longer than three sentences.

5. Track all of your blog submissions and build a list of high PR, do follow blogs that you can return to from time to time. Always leave comments on different posts—never the same post.

As someone who manages a blog and uses blog commenting on a regular basis to build one-way links to my sites, I know how important the above guidelines are for making the most of blog commenting.

When moderating comments for my own blog, I personally don't mind people using their keyword as the name (although some blogs won't allow this) and linking to their website in the URL field. In fact, I see it as a quid pro quo if they take the time to read my post and leave a valuable comment. However, I will delete their comment if they place a link in the body of the comment because it's usually SPAM.

Start searching for those blogs that can support your link building and be part of the conversation. You can add this strategy to the mix and start to see why link building can be fun and somewhat addictive.

Social Bookmarks

Social bookmarking is a way for Internet users to store, classify, share, and search Internet bookmarks. A number of years ago, social bookmarking sites such as Del.icio.us, Diigo, Furl, Ma.gnolia, Netvouz, and StumbleUpon became popular. Soon thereafter, sites like Reddit, Digg, and Newsvine began applying social bookmarking to news items, and now the concept of bookmarking is pervasive throughout the Internet. Many years later, the process of social bookmarking is alive and well. The concept itself is similar to "social media," but doesn't have the same level of flexibility or scope.

In simple terms, social bookmarking is a way of tagging content on the web (news, articles, web pages, etc.) for easy referencing by yourself and others who may be tagging the same content. This is very similar to using a bookmark when reading your favorite novel. The purpose is to make it easy to get back to where you left off or identify content you deem important. Social bookmarking works in much the same way. The only real difference is the social component—others can see your bookmarks and you can see theirs.

You can use social bookmarks in a variety of ways to build inbound links to your website and, therefore, improve your overall site popularity and Google SERPs. What I personally like about social bookmarking is it's easy to do and very similar to other optimization methods I use.

The practice of bookmarking works like this: A user registers for a social bookmarking site (example: Del.icio.us). Once he has an account, he browses the Internet. When the individual identifies a web page or piece of content he wants to share with others, he bookmarks or tags it by clicking a bookmarking icon. Once bookmarked, the bookmarking site keeps a record of the individual's bookmark and checks to see if others have selected the same content.

When others bookmark the same content, it increases in popularity and is ranked higher on the social bookmark site, allowing others to see the most popular web content as voted on by browsers from across the Internet. Some of these bookmark sites also let you view the bookmarks of others. Del.icio.us is famous for this; just type in the name of any celebrity and see what they've bookmarked (e.g., Pamela Anderson). That's what makes "social" bookmarking so much fun!

Bookmarking your own site on major social bookmarking websites is a great way to develop one-way links to your site and improve your Google results. I have found a great free tool, named *Social Poster* that makes posting to multiple bookmarking sites easy. Other sites like it can be found at socialposter.com/generator.php. Another site is Ping.fm, which provides the same type of functionality but automates the posting process once you've registered at all sites. This tool allows you to tag your site across multiple bookmarking sites instead of having to visit each one independently. You will need to register for each social bookmark site before bookmarking your own website.

After visiting these social bookmarking sites and bookmarking your homepage on each of them, consider bookmarking channel level pages of your site. Creating deep links into your site can enhance your overall Google rankings. And of course, make sure to use the proper link text in your site title and description.

One final word on social bookmarking: Now that you know how to bookmark your site, the next logical step is to make it easy for others to bookmark your own website. To do this, simply add a social bookmark applet (free) to your site by visiting http://AddThis.com. They offer a small piece of JavaScript you can add to your site in the form of a button.

When users click on the *Bookmark* button they can view a dropdown list of various social bookmarking sites and select their preferred bookmarking tool to select your web page. This makes the process of bookmarking simple and easy to do.

Over time, as more and more browsers bookmark your website, the number and quantity of bookmarks continue to increase. These bookmarks serve as inbound links to your website or web page, helping to boost Google SERPs.

Press Releases

One of the secrets I've used to get my link distributed on hundreds of websites, almost overnight, is through press release distribution. The way this technique works is by distributing a press release—an announcement of news related to your website—containing links back to your website. Now you might be saying, "Hey, I'm not in public relations and I know nothing about press releases." That's OK; you can use the press release template that I've developed by visiting www.myseomadesimple.com/secret.htm and distribute it to media outlets across the web containing links back to your website.

Now that Google displays universal search results, press releases and other forms of media appear on page one of Google results. In addition to using press releases to build inbound links to your website (from the press release sites and websites that pick up your release), you can also often get page one listings for a brief time.

I used this technique to promote affiliate web pages with a high degree of success. I needed to spin my releases and redistribute daily, but for a time it was very effective for driving traffic and conversions. When researching your keyword, take notice of the press release sites that appear on page one Google listings. Register for those sites and distribute your own releases through the same channels. Simple? Yes. Effective? Yes. Give it a try and you'll see why press releases are a great tool for improving your search engine rankings and website traffic!

Before distributing a release, consider the different types of releases you can create. The most valuable press releases are usually newsworthy and can stand on their own. When you share actual news, the likelihood of that information getting picked up by online news outlets and distributed to hundreds or even thousands of sites can quickly become a reality.

In my opinion the best way to create news is through an online poll or survey. Here are a couple of suggestions for creating a poll that is newsworthy and supports the press release strategy.

Option 1: If you're starting from scratch I recommend adding a poll question to your blog. The only reason I suggest adding it to your blog versus your website is that blogs usually offer tools like online polling with a single click. If you haven't started a blog yet, take five minutes to create one (including an online poll) at Blogger.com.

Option 2: If you have your own list (opt-in e-mails), use a tool like SurveyMonkey to develop a short survey and distribute it to your list. It will be the best $20 you ever spend. You can find more information on this survey solution at http://SurveyMonkey.com. As always, you can choose any survey solution as long as you have a predetermined list you can send it to. I would suggest leaving your poll or survey open until you've gotten at least one hundred responses. Preferably, you should target around 250, but one hundred should suffice for your first release. Once you've completed your first survey and written your press release, you can select an online press release distribution service. A variety of sources can distribute your press release and usually charge between $1 and $250.

Keep in mind that a press release is any bit of information that your prospective market would find of interest or value. For example, I've distributed releases when I launched my website and each time I collected information from an online poll. You could also distribute a press release each time you add a new feature to your site that delivers value or is unique to the market you serve.

Keep in mind that the primary purpose of your press release is to build links to your website. Although I've used this strategy to achieve page one rankings for a short time, the actual value is created when other sites link to your release, which in turn is linking to your own website or blog. This is what Google needs to recognize and rank your site. As a result, you want to select a distribution option where *your link is active and you can specify the link text.* As you learned earlier, you must include your keywords in the link text if you wish to succeed on Google. If the press release distribution option doesn't include an active link, meaning a link to your website, select a different option or service.

I have used PRWeb for distribution services with my own press releases. However, PRWeb can get a bit pricey. If you're just starting out and don't have the budget for a top-notch service, I recommend using PR-Inside or Free-Press-Release.com. They offer less distribution, but you can choose a more affordable option that lets you embed a link and specify anchor text. The key is to see which press release sites are already ranking in search results for your desired keyword phrases. Always make sure to use those sites which are currently generating listings on page one of Google search results.

Once distributed, give your release a few days to be picked up by the media and media outlets. The beauty of the press release is that "good news travels fast." After receiving initial media pickup, your release continues to be distributed for days and weeks to come. The press release, if newsworthy, is a fantastic tool for developing Google-friendly links.

RSS Feeds

Syndicating your own website content is a great way to provide information to your readers with little or no effort. Using an RSS feed, your updated content is delivered to individuals who have subscribed to your feed automatically and can include links back to your website and reprint instructions (remember, it's all about the links!).

RSS is a simple XML-based system that allows users to subscribe to their favorite websites. Using RSS, webmasters can put their content into a standard format that can be viewed and organized through RSS software or automatically conveyed as new content on another website.

A program known as a feed reader or aggregator can check a list of feeds on behalf of a user and display any updated articles that it finds. It is common to find web feeds on major websites and many smaller ones. Some websites let people choose between RSS or Atom-formatted web feeds.

Feeds are typically linked with the word *Subscribe*, an orange rectangle 🔊 or with the letters **RSS**. Many news aggregators publish subscription buttons for use on web pages to simplify the process of adding news feeds.

Choosing the Content You Want to Syndicate

OK, so you're interested in syndication but aren't exactly sure what you should be syndicating. There's really no hard and fast rule here. However, keep in mind that anything you plan to syndicate via RSS should be unique, of value to a given audience, and something that is updated on a regular basis.

Some individuals syndicate their content by placing an RSS feed on their homepage. As the website is updated and a new feed is produced, content is sent directly to subscribers. Others choose to provide a feed of specific content pages on their site. The choice is yours.

So How Do you Create an RSS Feed? All RSS feeds are written using a code type called XML. If you're not familiar with XML don't let that scare you. I'll provide the specific code you need and instructions on what to do with it.

To begin, you'll need to create an RSS file that contains a title, description, and link URL. This information will be used by the RSS reader when individuals subscribe to your RSS feed. I've created an RSS feed on my articles page allowing subscribers to receive new articles each time they are published. You can too—simply follow these steps.

1. Go to your *Start Menu* in the lower left-hand corner or your computer screen. Click on *All Programs* and navigate to *Accessories*. There you'll find an option called *Notepad*. Notepad is a simple text editor that you will use to develop your RSS script.

2. Write the RSS script, which contains information about your website or content page and information about the content you'll be syndicating. To do so, type the following into Notepad. Replace the bold content with your own website's information.

<?xml   version="1.0"   encoding="ISO-8859-1"   ?>   <rss version="0.91>

This RSS feed should be viewed using an RSS Reader or RSS Aggregator. Firefox users do this by clicking on the "Subscribe to feed" icon.

Feed URL: **http://www.marketingscoop.com/**

<channel>
<title>**Marketing Articles**</title>
<link>**http://www.marketingscoop.com/articles.htm**</link>
<description>**Marketing articles covering a variety of marketing topics**</description>
<language>en-us</language>
<copyright>**MarketingScoop.com**</copyright>

<item>
<title>**How to market your small business**</title>
<link>**http://www.marketingscoop.com/market-small-**

business.htm</link>

<description>**If you own a small business, you probably don't have a lot to spend on marketing. These simple techniques will help you generate more referrals than you can handle.**
</description>
</item>
</channel>
</rss>

That's it. As noted above, be sure to replace the content presented in bold type with your own. When you're done save your file by selecting *File* then *Save As* from the top bar in the Notepad window.

Note: Name your file with a .xml extension but save the file as text (e.g., http://www.marketingscoop.com/rssfeed.xml).

Be sure not to use any ampersands or quotes in your code as this may cause an error. XML requires ampersands to be replaced in the code with "&amp" and quotes with "&quot." The best advice I can give is just don't include quotes or ampersands and you won't have any coding issues.

3. Save, upload, and validate your .xml code. After saving your RSS file via Notepad, upload your .xml file to your web server. This file should be placed on the same directory as your homepage or the directory of the page you've selected to syndicate. Now that we've created and uploaded your RSS feed, we must validate it. By doing so, we know that the feed is active and will work when individuals subscribe. To validate your feed, visit http://validator.w3.org/feed and enter your feed URL. The URL of your feed is simply the URL of the .xml file you just uploaded to your server. If your file was saved to your website's main directory and was called *rssfeed*, simply enter your website's URL, followed by /rssfeed.xml. Once validated, your RSS feed is ready to be syndicated.

4. Place your RSS code on your website. The best way to do this is to copy an RSS button `RSS` and include a link to the RSS feed you just created. You can grab the RSS or XML image by simply visiting a website like MarketingScoop.com/articles.htm and right-mouse click the image. Save the image (give it a name like

RSS.gif) and copy it onto your server. The code should look like this:

```
<a href="http://www.yourwebsite.com/rssfeed.xml"> <img border="0" src="images/rss.gif" alt="rss feed for my website" width="36" height="14"></a>
```

As usual, replace the information above with your own feed link and image link.

5. Subscribe to your own feed. After you've uploaded all of your pages to your live site or testing server, open Internet Explorer and click on your own RSS button. You should be taken to a dialogue box that asks if you'd like to subscribe to your feed. Subscribe and confirm that the feed has been added to your list of RSS feeds (it should appear in a dialogue box on the left hand side of the page).

Note: If you're using Firefox, you will only receive a text page when clicking on your RSS button. Those using the Firefox browser can click on a small icon that resides on their browser navigation bar to add your feed. Additionally, the text file contains their feed URL, which can also be used.

6. Ping aggregators to let them know that you've created an RSS feed. In order to let the web know that your feed is up and running, you must give them a ping. This is very easy to do—just go to http://pingomatic.com and choose the appropriate sites to inform. Select blog-related sites if you're a blog and non-blog-related sites for other content. Complete the information and ping.

A final note: Whenever you want to syndicate new content, you'll need to update your .xml file with a link to the content and a revised description. Once you've done so, upload the file to your server, replacing the existing .xml file.

Another syndication service you can use is Feedblitz. I've implemented Feedblitz so that users can receive updates to my blog, article pages, and websites by registering with only a name and email address. Once subscribed, registrants receive an update via email each time I've added information to my blog or website. Feedblitz also offers syndication services. This is a great option if you are new to RSS feeds and would like to have your feeds accessible from a single location.

Forum Marketing

The Internet is an amazing place. If you have a question, about anything, you can usually find the answer online. This is especially true when it comes to search engine optimization, pay-per-click, and other forms of online marketing. In fact, when searching for an answer to a question via Google or any search engine, you're bound to find a listing for a blog post or forum post. Forums are essentially large communities where similar minded people share ideas, ask questions, and answer them too.

Forums have been around a long time. In fact, if you visit www.big-boards.com, you'll find thousands of forums listed. Many of these forums have tens of thousands of members. These communities are large and provide the type of interaction you need to answer any question on a particular topic. Forums have become so popular that I launched my own forum (Internet Marketing Forum) on my MarketingScoop.com website. You can find a link to the forum on my secret page or just Google "Internet marketing forum."

The benefit of having my own forum is that I can manage the conversation and take advantage of the many benefits of being a forum owner. However, you DON'T need to own a forum to benefit your search engine optimization.

How can you use forums to improve your rankings? The answer is quite obvious. You can use forums to generate inbound links to your websites and blogs. The question of how to do this is what we are focusing on.

The first step in any link-building initiative is to find a relevant forum and start posting. You can begin by doing a Google search or by using big-boards.com. There are a few things that you need to look for:

- Is the forum related to your niche?

- Is the forum well established? Is it new or has it existed for some time?

- Does the forum have a good Google PR?

- Does the forum seem active?

- Does the forum allow links in your signature? Are the links "do follow" links?

Once you have researched possible forums and created a list of at least ten that meet your criteria, it's time to register and start posting. Before you start posting there are a few things you'll need to take care of. The first is to register for the forum accepting the terms and conditions. This is usually a very simple process that may require a valid email and clicking on a confirmation link. Once complete, you can log into the forum and visit your control panel.

The control panel is the place on the forum where you can set up your preferences and your forum signature. All forums have a control panel which may be labeled as the "CP" or "Profile." This is the area where you control how your forum signature, what shows beneath each post, will appear. Keep in mind that many forums require you to make ten full posts before allowing your signature to show. This is due to the fact that more and more people are using forums to build third-party links to their websites, blogs, and affiliate offers.

Set up your signature to include a link to your website using a keyword phrase as your anchor text. Many signatures allow up to three links but I would limit your signature to two. Use the "|" symbol we discussed earlier so you can include two keyword phrases for each link. Once your signature is set up, it's time to start posting. Always check the box that says "display my signature" if available.

To make the most of your forum posting, find threads (questions and responses) about a topic on which you can comment. Having my own forum, I know that many of the posts can be of poor quality. When they are, my moderators may delete them. If you're going to leave a comment on the forum, make sure it's a good one. The more valuable your comments, the more staying power they'll have. Additionally, a number of forums have integrated social media opportunities. This means that if your question or response is of high quality, others may use social bookmarks to identify them or share via social media outlets like Twitter and Facebook. Similar to blog commenting, forum posts should be relevant, meaningful, and valuable. This gives your signature links the "link juice" you want.

Always pace your forum posting. The goal is to find ten relevant forums that you can actively contribute to on a monthly basis. I used to spend a lot of time in forums but found that forum posting—although extremely valuable—can be very time consuming as well. A few forum-posting tools out there can aid in making posts, but manual submissions are still the most powerful and require a little work.

I share some of my outsourcing strategies later in this guide. Outsourcing something like forum posting provides a really good return on your investment. My recommendation is to do the research, set up your profiles and make the initial posts on the most popular niche forums. Once you've completed that work you are in a great position to outsource your forum posting activities.

Caution: A lot of people assume that any time they want to promote a different website or change a signature for future posts they can simply log into their forum control panel and change their signature. The assumption is that changing their signature only affects future posts. This is often not the case. Changing your signature may impact all existing posts already submitted on the forum. As a result, it may be necessary to create multiple accounts so that you can have truly unique signatures that stand the test of time.

Getting Authority Links: Profile Sites

I actually learned about high authority profile sites by accident. In fact, if it weren't for my need to experiment, I'd likely have overlooked this effective SEO technique and never had the opportunity to share it with you in this book.

For a time I focused a lot of my energy on affiliate marketing. Even today I make a nice residual income with niche websites where I earn a commission each time a product or service is sold. A couple of years ago I started searching for new ways to sell my own products and generate traffic to my niche websites. In short order, I stumbled upon a forum that included "special offers" from other Internet marketers. I liked the idea so much that I even added this feature to my marketing forum! One of the special offers had to do with a list of high PR websites where you could leave a link back to your website.

I purchased the list and found a bit of a mixed bag. Some of the sites were no longer active or only allowed you to leave a link on a dynamic page—which has little value—but most of the sites noted were legitimate and carried a great deal of authority. Ever since I first discovered this technique of finding and dropping links on high PR sites, which I call Profile Sites, I've relied on monthly submissions to help my rankings.

The reason I call these sites Profile Sites is because they are often based on forums, social Media sites, wikis, and other online resources that allow you to include a link with your registration profile. Upon completing your registration, you can include a link that is immediately accessible or available when you leave some type of comment or post on the site itself.

The resource that I currently use, Angela's links (more information on where to find this fantastic resource and added bonuses at http://www.myseomadesimple.com/secret.htm), provides me with a fresh list of high PR sites each month for a nominal fee. The sites highlighted often include dot com and dot edu websites. Getting links from dot edu sites is very valuable and hard to come by. Having someone else do the research for you each month to find these authoritative sites is well worth the small investment. When leveraging high Profile Sites, you often get a diversity of authoritative links that you can use time and again. Due to the popularity of some of these sites, registration isn't always available. However, for everyone that closes, many more high PR sites become available.

A number of SEO tools that I've experimented with over the last year integrate profile sites into their process. They understand the value of getting one-way links from sites with authority. My recommendation is that you respect the submission guidelines for these sites when building links. Hitting the same sites again and again, with links pointing to the same third-party websites, may be recognized as spam.

Keep a spreadsheet of each of these sites and their status. I know that each time I launch a new site I keep going back to my list of high authority Profile Sites. You should do some research on authority websites, make a list, and always look for one-way links from registration profiles on high PR websites. Resources like Angela's links are invaluable.

Social Media Sites (including video)

Unless you've been living under a rock for the last few years, it's hard to ignore social media. It seems that every day existing social media sites are getting larger and new ones are cropping up all over the place. This popularity is driven by the viral nature of social media. You invite your friends, they invite their friends, and before you know it, the whole world is connected.

I've been participating in social media for a long time. A number of social media sites have come and gone over the years, but some continue to dominate the social media space. Facebook, Twitter, and YouTube are the leading contenders. Google and other search engines are putting their social media spin on things too and it's just a matter of time before their social networks are a large part of the mix.

By now you know that I have a one-track mind. That's certainly true when it comes to social media. One must ask the question, "How can I use social media sites to improve the ranking of my own websites and blogs?" There are two answers to that question and they are very much aligned to what we've been talking about in this section. The answer is "links" and "rankings."

Social media links are created when you develop a profile on a social media website like Facebook. If you have a Facebook account it likely includes links of various kinds—links to books you're reading, products you recommend, and hopefully links back to your websites or blogs. By the very nature of Facebook, it carries tremendous authority. If you are linking to your own website, it passes that authority back to you. When setting up your profile on Facebook, Twitter, and YouTube, you should always include at least one link back to your website and other digital assets.

Facebook. Let's begin with Facebook. Signing up and getting started with Facebook is very easy. Visit the home page and complete the basic information then click, "Sign Up." Once you register, confirm, and set up your profile, you'll be able to take advantage of everything Facebook has to offer. When registering, complete all aspects of your profile and seek guidance from friends who are currently using Facebook for tips and guidance on the numerous Facebook features. Learning what to do and how to do it from current users is definitely the quickest way to get up to speed.

Keep in mind that your profile name will be visible in Facebook, so choose your naming convention carefully. This is something you'll want to give some thought to. Don't worry though. In addition to setting up an account under your name, you'll also be able to create a company profile (Fan Page). This gives you added visibility and the opportunity to add links that point to your website. Additionally, you can post other links on your "Wall."

The true SEO value of Facebook is in building a network and asking others to post or share your links on their profile pages, Wall, or on their own digital assets, such as blogs and forums. Over time, your profile, and the links distributed by those in your network are what create SEO value.

Twitter. The concept of Twitter is pretty unique. After registering and setting up a profile, you create short posts of 140 characters or less online or using your cell phone. These posts are visible to everyone who is following you as well as those viewing a particular thread. Threads are visible using a hashtag. Hashtags are identified by the pound sign "#" and appear before a phrase (ex: #SEO). If I'm subscribed to "#SEO" for example, I'll be able to view anyone's Tweet that is followed with #SEO thanks to this hashtag feature.

Using Twitter for SEO is also a two-part process. The first part is to include a link to your website from your Twitter profile. After logging in to your profile, click on the "edit your profile link" and "Profile" from the top menu. You will see a location for your web address. Enter your URL there. Once you start building Twitter followers, and they link to your profile, this will improve the authority of this link.

The second way to use Twitter for SEO is to build a list of Twitter followers. You can do this by sharing your handle (example: @mfleischner) on your blog, in your marketing messages, on your website, and so on. You can also use some pretty neat tools that automate the following process for you, building a large list of followers relatively quickly. For a listing of the Twitter software I use to manage my Twitter account, visit my secret page. Many individuals set up automated following. That means if you follow them, they will follow you back. You can start following individuals of interest manually or use automated software to do so. Although I don't recommend this for everyone, if you are just starting out on Twitter, taking advantage of automated following is a great way to build a list quickly. Once you have a list of targeted followers, you can make them aware of valuable content and features available on your website. Always make your content easy to bookmark and share with others! Using Twitter to drive followers to your website is just the beginning. Once there, your site needs to force an action, moving them into a sales funnel or giving them the option to bookmark or share content.

It's essential that you consider what type of content you'll deliver on Twitter. I've built a following of more than ten thousand people by providing helpful SEO-related tips and strategies on a regular basis. Focus on your niche and "Tweet" about an area you know a lot about.

YouTube. Begin by creating an account. Once you register, you'll have a number of options available to you. Click on your username and select "Account." If you click on "Profile Setup" in the left margin, you'll see a place to enter your URL. In addition, each time you upload a video, you can enter a description. When writing your descriptions, always start with your URL in the beginning. Doing so makes the link visible and active.

One of the best ways to promote your video and, therefore, your link, is to tell others about it. YouTube has a subscribe option so once you learn more about YouTube and create a "channel," you can drive your visitors directly to your videos. Once there, visitors can take advantage of a number of rating options. You can also customize your channel with various features including comments, subscribers, and so on.

YouTube videos are ranked by the number of subscribers, "Likes," and comments. Whenever you produce a video, send a link to your list, post a link to the video on your site, and encourage users to comment. This can help your ranking in Youtube and may encourage third-party websites to embed the video directly into their content. Sharing and embedding videos means more links to the video itself, which in turn creates more link juice. Over time the number and quality of links pointing to your site, through your Youtube link, gain authority which helps your rankings.

If you've never created a YouTube video, don't despair. There is a great deal of quality video on YouTube and Vimeo that show you simple ways of creating professional looking videos. Spend some time learning the art of video making or just use your webcam. Publishing videos is relatively easy and video production doesn't need to be complicated. Once you know how to produce a simple video, you can fuel your link-building efforts in a powerful way.

Social media can be a great way to build quality third-party links that add value to your own website or blog by passing link authority to your digital assets. If you aren't actively engaged with social media, get started today. The sooner you become active with social media the faster you build authority and the more value you create for SEO.

Google Places (a.k.a. "Local")

Any SEO guide would be remiss if not mentioning Google Local. Google's localization strategy is in full force and seems to be integrated into more and more search results. Most people don't fully understand Google Places or realize how they can use "Local" to achieve first place listings and top placements.

The first step is to register for a Google Places account. Start by going to places.google.com and registering. When you do, complete as much information in your profile as possible. The key to showing at the top of a local search results isn't necessarily distance or an alphabetical listing. Google is searching for relevance.

Relevance is created with a comprehensive description of the services you offer. Even if you're an online business, you should be developing a Google Places profile and providing as much information as possible. Additionally, you'll want to take advantage of all the features provided by Google Places. This includes the ability to add photos, reviews, and videos. Google also allows you, using the Google Tags option, to provide special offers or coupons to those who visit your profile.

To optimize your Google Places profile, add as much content as possible. Repurpose videos you've created—no matter how basic. Add photos of your business. If your business is simply online, then add photos of your products, screenshots of your website, or any other pictures that are relevant to your business. The final step is soliciting reviews.

Online reviews are driving the Internet. Look at businesses like Amazon.com and it's clear that reviews are an essential part of any online or offline business. The best way to solicit reviews is to ask anyone of your satisfied clients to post a review. Make it easy for them by providing a link in a follow-up email or posting a message on your website. It's OK to have a mix of positive and negative reviews. This makes your business appear credible and people have come to expect positive and negative experiences with any business.

A quick word on ethics: Don't bother paying others to write reviews for you—it's dishonest. Personally, I have found that when you ask your customers to write reviews, you'll get plenty. And, the majority of the reviews will be positive. Instead of spending energy trying to bump up your reputation artificially, engage your customers and website visitors.

Using Google Places doesn't take a lot of work and is rather easy to implement. I'm sure you can buy a book or pay for a Google Places instructional program. Personally, I don't think Google Places is all that difficult to learn or use. Before you spend your money, register for an account and implement the techniques I've already mentioned.

Once your account is up and running, continually add content when appropriate and invite others to complete reviews. The more content you add to your listing (keyword rich of course) the higher your Google Places ranking will be, and the more link juice you'll receive.

Give People a Reason to Link to Your Website

One of the best ways to attract one-way links to your website is to promote free content, such as news or articles, white papers, free tools, and so on, via your own website or blog. This is the inverse of the link-building strategy we've been discussing where you actually push content to other websites or blogs. Using this strategy, you are creating valuable content and subscribing to that old adage, "If you build it, they will come." It might sound cliché, but thanks to social media and the web, you can attract users to your website (and links) by having something of value to offer. If you provide something of value, other websites will start linking to you, giving one-way links that can dramatically improve your search engine results.

Personally, I like to create article collections that provide a wealth of information to website browsers seeking information. For example, I've developed a posting of marketing-related articles that I have written during my professional career, placing them in a special free articles section of my website. There are a number of other websites linking to this resource, and as a result, I'm ranked number one for the terms *free marketing articles* and in *marketing article*—two highly trafficked and sought after terms in the marketing niche. I make sure to add new articles on a regular basis to keep the content fresh. Doing so encourages other sites to create links to the content from their own websites.

Another suggestion is the production of a small promotional ebook. If you've ever downloaded a book electronically from the World Wide Web, you already have experience with ebooks. When users know they can get something, even a small promotional ebook for free, they tell others. This creates a "viral" effect that is great for attracting one-way links.

If you can create an ebook of your own, regardless of its length, develop it in Word and save it as a PDF. As a last step, post it on your website and make available after browsers provide their name and email address. If you need help with your ebook or would like to leverage the work others have done, search for PLR-related materials. PLR stands for private label rights, and you can often "buy" the rights to completed ebooks, how-to manuals, and the like, for little or no money.

The next step is to offer these PLR ebooks on your website. Before long, others will be linking to you because you're providing something of value. Just make sure they are linking in the right way. On your web page, encourage people to link to your ebook and provide them with the proper link text (e.g., If you'd like to link to us, please use the following: <a href="http://www.yoursitename.com" title="your keyword phrase" rel="dofollow">Your keyword phrase</a>).

As I mentioned at the start of this section, off-page optimization is the most important factor for improving Google SERPs. Use the *SEO Made Simple* techniques to build quality links to your website and watch your search engine rankings soar!

All of these off-page optimization techniques, when applied consistently over time, significantly improve Google SERPs and results on other major search engines. After implementing the various off-page optimization methods we've covered, select those you are most comfortable with and apply on a regular basis.

Outsourcing

After many years of creating content, optimizing websites, and spending countless hours building links to my many websites and blogs, a good friend and Internet guru turned me on the concept of outsourcing. Personally, I never really trusted anyone with my web properties or SEO and still tread lightly. However, over the past couple of years I have found a couple of good outsourcing partners that I use to support the search engine optimization of my own websites and blogs – and so can you.

The concept of outsourcing is simple. Find resources to do repetitive or time-consuming tasks at a low cost. While they are focusing on "getting it done," you can focus on new projects, revenue-generating activities, and other work.

I used to think that outsourcing was only for large companies. To be honest I had many false perceptions about outsourcing and the types of individuals that support outsourcing-related jobs. The reality is that you can find a number of highly qualified, intelligent individuals who are willing to complete work at a much lower cost than it would be in your own country. I've used freelancers in India,

Sweden, and the Philippines for programming, link building, and administrative tasks.

Whether you are working on a single website or twenty, I recommend learning more about the opportunity to outsource specific tasks. There are a variety of resources that allow you to find just the right person to support your SEO. My personal favorites are oDesk, eLance, and UpwardSEO.com. There are many others available such as Getafreelancer.com and Guru.com but I'm partial to the first few because of their size and my personal experience with them.

Here's how outsourcing for a typical SEO project might work. You begin by defining tasks that you want to complete on a weekly or monthly basis. After creating a list, spend some time thinking about what you can handle on your own and on what you will need support. Said another way, what should you pay to have someone else do versus doing yourself?

By spending time up front to determine which tasks should be outsourced and which you can handle on your own, you are more likely to choose the right outsource partner. Investing quality time in this process will pay huge dividends down the line.

As an example, let's say that you want to outsource forum posting or blog posting. The first thing you have to ask yourself is how effective an outsourcing partner can be with either of these tasks. For me, I'd say that forum posting is probably easier for an international person than blog posting. Blog commenting requires an individual to read a blog post (in a language they understand), find an entry to comment on, and write a well-articulated response in the appropriate language. This increases your chances of having a comment "stick" and therefore requires some level of expertise.

Forum posting, from my perspective, requires some of the same skills as blog commenting, but not always. I could likely find dozens of IT-related blogs that talk about programming languages and anyone with a little HTML or php experience could write a post or comment on a thread. Seek out an outsource partner who has experience with forum posting in general and specific content knowledge to be effective.

While they are doing the heavy lifting on forum postings every month, I'll focus on other high-value SEO tactics like article writing and article spinning which requires a native speaker and someone with a good grasp of the subject matter. Article writing, spinning, and distribution are best done "in house." But seeking out tools to help you with this process is advised (www.myseomadesimple.com/secret.htm). Between outsourcing and the use of semi-automated tools you can dramatically reduce the time it takes you to complete optimization activities.

Once you have a list of tasks that you want to outsource, it's time to find a provider. If you have programming needs I recommend using eLance.com. There you can post a project and have multiple providers bid on your job. Read through reviews, samples of work, and so on to determine which vendor can best meet your needs. Overall I've had a very positive experience with eLance and the providers available through their network. That doesn't necessarily guarantee success. My advice is to approach outsourcing as a work in progress. Keep experimenting with different vendors until you find the perfect match. In time you'll have a short list of affordable vendors you can use for virtually anything web related.

If you are looking for freelancers who can support your search engine optimization activities like link building, I recommend using Upward SEO or oDesk. Start with a clear understanding of what you need done, by when, and at what price. Both sites offer a very robust search that helps you narrow down candidates rather quickly. Contact the individuals you are considering and ask them to do a small assignment for you. If they are successful, consider hiring them on a regular basis. Again, this takes some work, patience, and experimentation. Once you find a valuable resource, you'll lighten your burden and increase productivity at the same time.

As your business grows and you know more about SEO, I highly recommend outsourcing. It does take some initial work and research to find the perfect outsourcing partner, but I've found qualified programmers for as little as $15/hr, and individuals to help with SEO tasks related to my own sites for less than $4/hr. Not only is the quality of work excellent, but affordable as well. This allows me to focus on bigger and better projects and have more free time to spend with family and friends—a real priority in my life.

Caution: Automated Tools, Shortcuts, and Other SEO Blunders!

Now that I've shared the link-building methods I've used to successfully achieve top search engine rankings, and build a number of online businesses, I thought I'd cover some of the do's and do not's you should consider when implementing any search engine optimization campaign.

For starters, let me remind you that this is a marathon not a sprint. This is something I've shared with all of my consulting clients who either expect instant results or don't have a full grasp on how search engine optimization works.

If you want page one listings in twenty-four hours, I can do that for you. All I would need to do is find a keyword phrase that isn't all that competitive and shows listings for press releases, articles, or social media on page one of Google. Then I'd put a link on my high authority blog with the keyword in the title or send out a press release from a site that already displays a result on page one. But what's the point? Once indexed, the corresponding listing will be there for three to five hours and then vanish as quickly as it arrived. SEO is not about creating a flash in the pan but rather applying search engine optimization best practices that result in top rankings that last with little or no maintenance. If you can accomplish that goal, everyone wins.

To get to the top you must pace your link-building efforts. In the next section, I'll actually show you how to do this. Again, build links too quickly and you'll get penalized. Build them methodically over time, and in the right way, and you'll achieve lasting results. Always keep the long-term in mind when it comes to SEO. I can tell you from years of SEO experience that when you start an active link-building campaign you may experience what's known as the "Google Dance." This is when you see your results shoot up one day, disappear the next, and bounce from position to position. This is actually a good sign. It means that Google is acknowledging your link-building activity and trying to award your site with an appropriate search position. Also remember that it's common to see little movement during the first few weeks or months of link building. Stay the course though. Upward movement of search position can happen quickly and significantly. Often times you have to prime the pump before you see results. All I can say is have faith in the methodology because it works. Optimizing your web pages and building quality inbound links produces results.

The other area to consider is link diversity. More often than not, you are going to find one link-building technique that you prefer above all others. This is natural and occurs with almost everyone. Nonetheless, you have to remember that Google is not just looking for inbound links; they are also looking at link diversity. You need to focus on attracting links of all kinds, not just a specific kind. Articles, blogs, forums, etc. all matter. Always seek to build a diverse set of inbound links versus putting all your eggs in one basket. If you were to focus on a single link type and Google changed their algorithm and devalued those links, your SEO efforts would become meaningless. Spread the risk and show Google that sites of all kinds are linking to your online resources.

One area that you should always be cautious of is full SEO automation. As mentioned previously, I've experimented with link building automation tools, and nine out of ten times they hurt your rankings. Either the tools themselves are flawed or, if functional, they can easily be misused. Don't fall prey to the dozens of vendors who promise search engine optimization automation. I confess that I do use a few automated tools but in a very limited way—to help me manage the dozens of websites and blogs I'm optimizing for at any one time. However, none of these tools handle 100% of the task. Rather, they are semi-automated and require interaction.

Some automated tools, which are more focused on keyword research or monitoring, are safe to use. For example, the one automated tool I do use religiously is Google Alerts. Set up alerts by visiting Google.com/alerts to see which sites are picking up and posting your content. Keyword research tools are also very helpful for reducing the time it takes to select strong keywords for your optimization efforts. You can see all of the tools I approve on my secret page.

The final area of caution is trying to be a lone ranger. When I started in SEO there wasn't much of an SEO community. Today, tens of thousands of people either make a living with search engine optimization or at least participate in SEO-related discussions on a regular basis. I encourage you to reach out to others in the community via forums and other online resources to ask questions and join the discussion. This is why I created the Internet Marketing Forum—to help streamline and build your knowledge of Search with like-minded individuals.

Section Two Summary

Here's what you should take away from this section about off-page optimization:

- ✓ Off-page optimization is your key to Google success.

- ✓ Your success on Google is based on which websites are linking to you and how they link to you.

- ✓ Link quality is essential for improving SERPs.

- ✓ When engaging in a reciprocal link, make sure that the website that is providing a link back to you has an equal or greater Google PR. This is important for maintaining a favorable Google PR balance.

- ✓ There are essentially three types of links: one-way, reciprocal, and three-way linking. One-way links, especially if they are from a page with a high Google PR, are the best.

- ✓ The most effective way to identify the right sites to get links from is to identify who is linking to your competition. You can do this by using search engine optimization software or by using major search engines.

- ✓ Sources for identifying inbound links to competitors include Google, Alexa, and SEO tools.

- ✓ Use the proper link text when link building.

- ✓ Always include your keywords and/or keyword phrases in your link text.

- ✓ When link building, remember that quality attracts quality.

- ✓ Be persistent, take massive action, and the links will come.

- ✓ Build your inbound links with the help of:

- article marketing
- link exchanges/link requests
- directory submissions
- blogging
- social bookmarks
- press releases
- RSS feeds
- forum marketing
- authority links
- social media sites
- Google places

✓ Give people a reason to link to your website.

✓ Use outsourcing to free up your time and complete repetitive
tasks.

✓ Be cautious of some automated link building tools as they can negatively impact your website ranking.

Section 3

Research to Practice

Link-Building Process

After writing the first edition of this book, I received literally hundreds of emails asking for more information and more insight into how I handle link building for my own websites and blogs. Based on the information you've read so far, you understand the importance of slow and steady link building. In fact, link-building cowboys are out there every day trying to get hundreds or thousands of links to their sites through automated services and shortcuts only to find that Google slaps them with a big penalty—setting their SEO back weeks or even months.

I've experimented with tons of paid services to support my search engine optimization efforts. Nine times out of ten, they either can't deliver what they promise or worse yet, have a negative impact on search results (ex: website submission services).

In this section, I'm going to reveal the exact link-building science I've applied to achieve number one rankings for many of my websites and blogs. And, it all begins with a very simple spreadsheet:

Site Name - Month		
Task	Date	Initials
One article spun and distributed (500+ sites)	MM/DD/YY	
25 directory submissions	MM/DD/YY	
10 do follow blog submissions	MM/DD/YY	
20 forum submissions	MM/DD/YY	
25 profile submissions	MM/DD/YY	
1 press release	MM/DD/YY	
5 social media links	MM/DD/YY	
3 video submissions	MM/DD/YY	
25 bookmarks per month	MM/DD/YY	

From my perspective, link building is a monthly process. Build links too quickly and you'll be penalized or perhaps achieve top rankings for only a short while (e.g., press releases). Build links too slowly and your competition may always outrank you. Striking the perfect balance takes experience and experimentation. I've spent a decade creating a link-building process that can give you the results you're looking for. The only variable is the competitiveness of your niche. I recently completed an SEO job for a well-known trucking company who wanted top rankings for a particular keyword phrase. This competitive phrase got nearly thirty thousand searches a month and had some very stiff competition. Although the company knew it would take a long time to achieve results, they understood the value in achieving a top ranking for this term. We applied the necessary SEO techniques and got the result they were looking for—but it took almost nine months. This is because the term was very competitive and other sites that were in the top positions had been there for a very long time. This is why doing the keyword research up-front, to find less competitive terms, is so important.

Once you have developed a website or blog, identified the keyword phrase you want to rank well for, and implemented on-page optimization, the next step is to have a link-building plan. Start your link building by developing a comprehensive list of sites linking into the top few results for the keyword phrase you're targeting. Systematically work through all those links and try to acquire links back to your site from each of them. Once your list has been exhausted, it's time for a disciplined link-building program.

The best way to manage your activity is by creating a spreadsheet that allows you to track your activity. The previous image is a summary level but you should also create tabs on your spreadsheet that capture the sites you use for submission. This allows you to come back to authoritative sites on a monthly basis and reuse them for link submissions.

Your plan should be as follows:

1. Create, spin, and distribute one article per month. Each article should include a link or two back to your site in the author section and possibly in the article itself. Consider using tools to help with this initiative. Use a spinner to create unique versions of your article and distribution resources. I usually have one or two articles per site queued up, spun, and ready to go at the beginning of each month. I distribute these articles at a pace of around fifty per day to potential directories and sites using semi-automated article distribution tools.

2. Submit to high PR web directories. Directory submissions are another great way to produce one-way links to your websites and blogs. Pace your submission, but don't worry about being too aggressive. Even if you submit to say twenty-five to fifty directories in a given month, most will take time to post your link, if at all. There is only a small success rate unless paying for a directory listing. Therefore, feel free to submit to a number of directories during the course of a month. Over time it will appear as though you are receiving a good number of directory listing confirmations on a regular basis.

3. Do follow blog submissions. Each month, focus on making quality submissions to "do follow" blogs in your niche. If you are unable to find do follow blogs in your niche, focus on high PR blogs of any kind. By taking the time to read posts and make value-added comments in the proper way, you can drive quality links to your site. I recommend no more than ten to twenty quality blog posts in a given month. Assuming you have a list of ten quality blogs each month, making a couple of posts on each should be easy. This also keeps things manageable. With most blogs there is moderation. As a result, your comments may take some time to appear live or may be rejected. Stay the course and you'll find more and more of your comments being accepted.

4. Forum submissions. As discussed previously, forum submissions are a great resource for one-way links. Keep in mind that you may need to make a minimum of ten posts before you are allowed to display your signature including links back to your website. Begin to register and cultivate a number of forums that you can go back to on a monthly basis to add content and display your signature. I suggest anywhere around twenty forum posts per month. The reason is that forum posting, much like blog posting, takes time. If you're aggressive you could certainly use forum posting much more. I'd shoot for around fifty posts in a month. This is definitely one of those tasks I'd consider outsourcing once you've established yourself on some targeted forums for your niche.

5. Profile submissions. Each month I use a freelancer to post on high-profile websites. Although Angela's packet offers around thirty potential links each month, invariably the list boils down to around twenty or so sites where you can easily place a one-way link back to your website. I use this list for all of the sites I'm optimizing and have even added my own list of high-profile sites that I revisit monthly. Again, if just starting out, try for about ten high-PR profile submissions for your site each month. If more advanced and you have supplemented the sites provided on Angela's list, you can post up to fifty over the course of a month. Once you've posted your link for a particular site on one of the suggested profile sites, do not post again until the following month. Duplicate links created at the same time won't help you and in fact may hurt your link-building efforts.

6. Press Release Submission. Each month you should be distributing one press release per website. Much like our article submission process, I like to write a release of around 350 words and put it into my spinner. Then, I make submissions to my list of top five free PR sites (e.g., Pr-inside, Free-Press-Release.com, PRlog.org, etc.). Once you have submitted to a press release distribution site, the news is distributed to hundreds of additional websites, news sites, and blogs.

7. Social Media Links. Social media is an important resource for communicating with others and posting links to your websites and blogs. Facebook, LinkedIn, Twitter, and the like, are common social media sites that you should be registered for and posting to on a regular basis. Include a link to your site in actual social media posts each month. The links in your profile are what matter most, but additional links on your "Wall" and in your "Tweets" can build link equity.

8. Video Submissions. I used to have video submissions and social media tied together for link-building purposes, and to a large extent, they are connected. YouTube, a video hosting site, is really one of today's largest social media sites. My goal is to produce one new video every month and post on video sites such as YouTube, Vimeo, and Viddler. Videos are commonplace and are easy to distribute. Additionally, universal search results are picking up and display videos in search result listings. Always make sure to include a link to your site in the beginning of your video's description when submitting to video sites.

9. Social Bookmarking. The concept of bookmarking is very powerful and one I've come to rely on for creating and managing inbound links across public websites. There are so many social bookmarking sites that you can do about twenty-five social bookmarks per month for a year and never hit the same site twice.

In the social bookmarking section I mentioned some resources for helping with your social bookmarking. Choose a strategy and post to social bookmarking sites on a monthly basis. I recommend not only bookmarking your home page URL but top level pages too. This is seen as less "spammy" and gives you many more pages to work with, avoiding duplicate bookmarks. Always use your keywords in the bookmarking link.

There you have it. This is the exact schedule, with minor tweaks from time to time, that I use on a monthly basis to optimize my own websites and blogs. I suggest that you spend the first few month of your SEO campaign working through each of the submission types on your own. Once you have a strong understanding and foundation for your link-building efforts, find an outsource partner that can help you with different aspects of the process. Before you know it, you'll be able to reduce the time you spend with repetitive tasks and focus on your next big search engine optimization project!

Conclusion

Increasing your ranking on Google and other search engines isn't complex, but it does take effort. If you want to increase your website ranking on search engine results pages, begin by implementing the on-page optimization and the off-page optimization techniques you've learned in this book.

One question I seem to get quite often is, "How long does it take?" This is a difficult question to answer because it's relative. If you're trying to optimize for a keyword phrase like "eating blueberries on a Sunday afternoon," it will happen quickly, requiring simple on-page optimization and just a few articles with links back to your website.

On the other hand, if you are trying to optimize for a competitive term, and the top-ranked website has hundreds of incoming links, it can take a number of months to reach number one on Google. I can tell you from experience that more often than not, you'll put in a lot of effort and it will appear as nothing is happening or only small shifts in results are occurring. But stay focused. All of a sudden...wham! Your site will jump up in the search results unexpectedly. Stay the course and I guarantee you'll see results.

Many fail because they give up too soon.

Regardless of where you're starting from, the key is persistence. These are the same techniques I've used to achieve top positions on Google for almost every keyword and keyword phrase that is important to my websites. Visualize your goal and take deliberate steps toward improving your search engine result placements daily and before long you will be exactly where you want to be—dominating the world's largest search engine.

To simplify your journey toward the number one position on Google, don't hesitate to use online effective SEO tools and resources and continue learning. Although search tools, including outsourcing, aren't required for achieving top search engine placement, they can help you reach your goal more quickly than manually implementing particular SEO techniques. Follow the strategies defined in this book; they've been proven effective by many individuals who have already begun using these techniques. I wish you the best of luck on your SEO journey. See you at the top and don't forget to always keep it simple!

A Simple Request

Thank you for reading, *SEO Made Simple*, 2nd Edition. If you feel this book has provided value, please visit Amazon.com and write a review.

I'm always looking for feedback and would love for you to be part of the SEO community. I will provide anyone who completes a review with access to my SEO training videos (a $297 value) absolutely FREE! Simply send a link to your review once posted on Amazon.com to support@myseomadeimple.com.

Section 4

SEO Glossary

Glossary

Below are some of the most common SEO-related words, phrases, and definitions. Some fellow authors who have reviewed my book in the past have said that I've wasted valuable space in these pages with an SEO glossary. I have to disagree. The glossary remains for the simple fact that I've heard from literally hundreds of individuals who appreciate the reference and use it on an ongoing basis. For more SEO-related definitions that can help you improve your knowledge of search engine optimization, visit the expanded marketing glossary online at http://www.marketingscoop.com/glossarylisting.aspx.

Affiliate marketing - An online marketing strategy that involves revenue sharing between online advertisers and online publishers. Compensation is typically awarded based on performance measures such as sales, clicks, registrations, or a combination of factors.

Alt tag - The alternative tag that the browser displays when the individual does not want to or cannot see the pictures present in a web page. Using alt tags containing keywords can improve the search engine ranking of the page for those keywords.

Alt text - Short for alternative text, it is used with an image and has a number of purposes. Primarily it is a placeholder for an image, so that if the image is slow to load or not shown, there will be an indicator of the content.

Anchor - Refers to a link on a web page, often found at the top or bottom of the page that allows users to move to specific content on the web page.

Anchor tag - Code determining the destination of a link.

Anchor text - The text part of any link, and of vital importance to any SEO effort. Instead of a link being displayed as www.marketingscoop.com, for example, using anchor text will allow the same link to be displayed as *Marketing Expert*. The search engines will then index the page based on this keyword.

Backlink - A link from one site that points to another. When getting backlinks, always ask the person linking to you to use anchor text.

Banner ad - A graphic Internet advertising tool. Users click on the graphic to be taken to another website or landing page. Banner ads are typically 468 pixels wide and 60 pixels tall, but the term can be used as a generic description of all online graphic ad formats.

Black hat - The use of unscrupulous methods to optimize a website. Discovery of these methods being used will often lead to a site being banned from major search engines.

Blog - A contraction of the term *weblog*, it is a form of Internet communication that combines a column, diary, and directory with links to additional resources.

Blogroll - A term used to describe a collection of links to other weblogs. Blogrolls are often found on the front-page sidebar of most weblogs. Various weblog authors have different criteria for including other weblogs on their blogrolls.

Browser - An individual searching the Internet for information. Also, a software package (Internet browser) used to view pages on the World Wide Web.

Caching - A computer process that stores web files to your computer for later access. These web pages are displayed without the need to re-download graphics and other elements of the previously visited page.

Canonical page - The preferred version of a set of pages with highly similar content.

Canonical tag – Html used to specify a canonical page to search engines. This is done by adding a <link> element with the attribute rel="canonical" to the <head> section of the non-canonical version of the page.

Cascading style sheets (CSS) - Used to manipulate and easily manage the design of a website.

Click - Each time a visitor clicks on a website or website link.

Click fraud - A form of theft perpetrated against advertisers who are paying per click for traffic, in which fraudsters may use automated means to click on your ads from spoofed IP addresses over random periods of time.

Click-through – A term used to measure the number of users who clicked on a specific Internet advertisement or link.

Click-through rate - The number of click-throughs per online ad impression, expressed as a percentage or exposure; a click on a link that leads to another website.

Click tracking - The use of scripts in order to track inbound and outbound links.

Cloaking - One of the most popular black hat methods, in which the visitor to the site is shown a page optimized to his search request, while the search engine spiders see a completely different set of pages designed to rank well.

Conversion rate - The percentage of targeted prospects that take a specified action within a given time frame.

Cookie - Computer code that is embedded in your Internet history file, allowing websites to recognize you as a returning visitor.

Cost-per-click - A specific type of cost-per-action program where advertisers pay each time a user clicks on an ad or a weblink.

Cost per thousand (CPM) - A simple and commonly used method of comparing the cost effectiveness of two or more alternative media vehicles. It is the cost of using the media vehicle to reach one thousand people or households.

Crawler - A program that goes through websites and gathers information for the crawler's creator.

Dead link - A link that produces a 404 error, page not found.

Deep linking - Connecting to a web page other than a site's homepage.

Deep submitting - Submitting all of your website's URLs—in other words, every page of your site—to a search engine. Most search engines forbid this practice.

De-listing/de-indexing - If search engines detect that you are using unscrupulous methods to get your site ranked, or if they regard your site as "spammy," they will remove your site from their index and it will no longer appear when users search for it.

Directory - A database of websites. Yahoo! and Open Directory are major examples. They are similar to search engines, except that the database is organized in a meaningful way by human beings. Many search engines use a directory as well as their own robots.

Domain name - The name assigned to a particular website (e.g., MarketingScoop.com).

Doorway page - A web page with content that's meaningful or visible only to the search engines; also called a *bridge page* or a *gateway page*.

Dynamic page - A page that generates content "on-the-fly" as a user requests the page.

eCommerce - An Internet-based business model that incorporates various elements of the marketing mix to drive users to a website for the purpose of purchasing a product or service.

Gateway page - A method once used to enable a site to rank well for a variety of keywords. It is frowned upon by the search engines and is no longer useful, as the search engines now base much of their algorithms on linking strategies.

Google - One of the most important spidering search engines by far, Google plays a dominant role in the search engine market.

Googlebot - The crawlers that index pages into Google.

Google Places – Previously referred to as Google Local. A search that produces local results based on proprietary algorithm.

Google Preview – The ability see a website thumbnail image from the primary search page of a Google search result.

HTML – Stands for *hypertext markup language*. The coded format language used for creating hypertext documents on the World Wide Web and controlling how web pages appear.

HTML e-mail - An e-mail that is formatted using hypertext markup language, as opposed to plain text.

Header tag - An HTML tag that is commonly used for page headers.

Hidden text - Text that is invisible to the human eye because it is the same color as the background.

Hit - When a person visits a web page, that web page receives a number of *hits*—one hit for the page itself, and one for every graphic on the page. The number of hits is not regarded as an accurate measurement of a website's popularity.

Hit rate - Also considered the conversion rate, it is the percentage of the desired number of outcomes received by a person relative to the total activity level.

Homepage - The main page of a website.

Impressions - The actual number of people who've seen a specific web page. Impressions are sometimes called *page views*.

Inbound link - A link from another website to your website.

Indexing - Behind-the-scenes creation of an ever-changing database based on the contents of web documents; search engines and filtering software use indexing to find and/or block documents containing certain words or phrases.

Internet - A worldwide network of computer networks. It is an interconnection of large and small networks around the globe. The Internet began in 1962 as a computer network for the U.S. military and over time has grown into a global communication tool.

IP address - A unique number that identifies a computer or system.

ISP - Short for *Internet service provider*, an ISP is a company that provides access to the Internet.

JavaScript - A scripting language developed by Netscape and used to create interactive websites.

Keyword - A word that is entered into the search form or search "window" of an Internet search engine to search the web for pages or sites about or including the keyword related to it.

Keyword density - Keywords as a percentage of text words that can be indexed.

Keyword marketing - Placing a marketing message in front of users based on the keywords they're using to search.

Keyword stuffing - Placing excessive keywords into page copy and coding such as meta tags; this may hurt the usability of a page but is meant to boost the page's search engine ranking. Hiding keywords on a page by making them the same color as the page background and loading tags with repeated keyword phrases are examples.

Keyword weight - Refers to the number of keywords appearing in the page area divided by the total number of words appearing in that area. Weight also depends on whether the keyword is a single word or a multi-word phrase.

Lead generation - The process of collecting contact information and identifying potential sales leads.

Link checker - A tool used to check web pages for broken links.

Link farm - A series of websites linking to each other in order to increase rankings.

Link popularity - Often used as one of the criteria to determine rank on search engines, the measure of the quantity and quality of sites that link to your website.

Meta search engine - A search engine that displays results from multiple search engines.

Meta tags - HTML coding that is used to describe various features of a web page and appears in search result listings.

Navigation - Elements of a website that facilitate movement from one page to another.

Online marketing - A term referring to the Internet and e-mail-based aspects of a marketing campaign, which can incorporate banner ads, e-mail marketing, SEO, eCommerce, and other tools.

Open Directory Project (DMOZ) - A large directory of websites run by volunteers. Their database is used by many websites across the Internet.

Opt-in - A program where membership is restricted to users who specifically request to take part.

Opt-out - A program that assumes inclusion unless stated otherwise. The term also refers to the process of removing one's name from a program.

Optimization - Fine-tuning a website or web page with the ultimate goal being to ascertain a higher position in all or a specific search engine's results.

Organic listings - Listings that appear on a search engine solely because of merit, applicability, etc. In other words, listings that are not paid for; also called *natural listings*.

PageRank - Part of Google's search algorithm, it measures a page's popularity and is calculated in part by analyzing the number of links to a page from other sites and factoring in the importance of those pages. The highest rank is a score of 10 out of 10.

Page view - A request to load a single HTML page. Indicative of the number of times an ad was potentially seen or *gross impressions*. Page views may overstate ad impressions if users choose to turn off graphics (often done to speed browsing).

Paid inclusion - Paying to be included in a search engine or a directory index. May not improve search rankings but guarantees inclusion of pages a spider might have missed and "respidering" of pages periodically.

Pay-per-click - An online advertising payment model in which payment is based solely on qualifying click-throughs.

Pay-per-sale - An online advertising payment model in which payment is based solely based on qualifying sales.

Pop-under - An online advertisement that displays in a new browser window behind the current browser window and is seen when an individual closes his current browser window.

Pop-up - An online advertisement that displays in a new browser window without an overt action by the website user.

Popularity - One of several criteria used by search engines to determine ranking in search results.

Public relations - The form of communication management that seeks to make use of publicity and other unpaid forms of promotion to influence feelings, opinions, or beliefs about the company, its products, or services.

Query - A search phrase submitted to search engines.

Ranking - The position of your website within the search engine indexes for a particular keyword.

RSS - Stands for *really simple syndication*. A lightweight XML format designed for sharing headlines and other web content. Typically, an RSS newsreader or aggregator is used to subscribe to syndicated RSS feeds.

Reciprocal links - An agreement where two website administrators agree to link to each other's websites.

Refresh tag - A tag that defines when and to where a page will refresh.

Robot - Any browser program that follows hypertext links and accesses web pages but is not directly under human control. Examples are the search engine spiders, the "harvesting" programs that extract data from web pages.

Robots.txt - If you wish to control which parts of your site a search engine spider indexes, you can use a robots.txt file to prevent the spider from indexing certain parts. Not all spiders will follow it, but it can be a useful tool if parts of your site are not ready for indexing.

SEO - Stands for *search engine optimization*. The process of developing a marketing and technical plan to ensure high rankings across multiple search engine results lists.

SERP - Stands for *search engine results placement*. Essentially, where your website is ranked on a given search engine for a chosen search term.

Search engine - A server or a collection of servers dedicated to indexing Internet web pages, storing the results, and returning lists of pages that match particular queries. The indexes are normally generated using spiders.

Search engine submission - The act of supplying a URL to a search engine in an attempt to make a search engine aware of a site or page.

Shopping cart - Software used to make a website's product catalog available for online ordering, allowing visitors to select, view, add/delete, and purchase merchandise.

Site search - A program providing search functionality across a single website or blog.

Skyscraper - A type of online ad that varies from a traditional banner size (468 x 60) and is significantly taller than the 120 x 240 vertical banner.

Social Media – Online resources developed for interaction among individuals using highly accessible and scalable publishing techniques. Social media uses web-based technologies to turn communication into interactive dialogues.

Spam - Unwanted, unsolicited e-mail, typically of a commercial nature.

Spider - A program that visits and downloads specific information from a web page.

Splash page - A branding page before the homepage of a website.

Stickiness - The amount of time spent at a website, often a measure of visitor loyalty.

Submission - Putting forward a site to a search engine or directory.

Thumbnail - A rough sketch or snapshot, usually of a website, that provides a small view of what a web page looks like in the form of a .jpg, .gif, or .png file.

Title tag - HTML code used to define the text in the top line of a web browser; also used by many search engines as the title of search listings.

Traffic - The visitors and page views on a website.

URL - Stands for *uniform resource locator*, an address that specifies the location of a file on the Internet.

Unique visitors - A measurement of website traffic that reflects the number of real individuals who have visited a website at least once in a fixed time frame.

Universal search - The integration of various media types into search result listings, including but not limited to websites, blogs, video, news, etc.

Viral marketing - A phenomenon that facilitates and encourages people to pass along a marketing message about a specific product, service, or company.

Web analytics - The process of using web metrics to extract useful business information.

Web browser - A software application that allows for the browsing of the World Wide Web.

Web design - The practice of selecting and coordinating available components to create the layout and structure of a web page.

Web directory - An organized, categorized listings of websites.

Web metrics - Statistics that measure different aspects of activity that transpire on a website.

Website - A site (location) on the World Wide Web. Each website contains a homepage, which is the first document users see when they enter the site. The site might also contain additional documents and files. Each site is owned and managed by an individual or company.

White hat - A reference to proper SEO methods that are approved by the search engines. Using these methods increases your chances of your site being permanently indexed in the search engines.

Whois - A utility that returns ownership information about second-level domains.

World Wide Web - A portion of the Internet that consists of a network of interlinked web pages.

XML feed - Simplified version of HTML that allows data (including product databases) to be sent to search engines in the format they request.

Notes: